Preparing for the Unimaginable

How chiefs can safeguard officer mental health before and after mass casualty events

First published in 2013 by the Office of Community Oriented Policing Services.
First Skyhorse Edition 2018.

Skyhorse Publishing books may be purchased in bulk at special discounts for sales promotion, corporate gifts, fund-raising, or educational purposes. Special editions can also be created to specifications. For details, contact the Special Sales Department, Skyhorse Publishing, 307 West 36th Street, 11th Floor, New York, NY 10018 or info@skyhorsepublishing.com.

Skyhorse® and Skyhorse Publishing® are registered trademarks of Skyhorse Publishing, Inc.®, a Delaware corporation.

Visit our website at www.skyhorsepublishing.com.

10 9 8 7 6 5 4 3 2 1

Library of Congress Cataloging-in-Publication Data is available on file.

Cover design by Office of Community Oriented Policing Services
Cover photo credit: Office of Community Oriented Policing Services

ISBN: 978-1-5107-2613-0
Ebook ISBN: 978-1-5107-2625-3

Printed in China

Preparing for the Unimaginable

How chiefs can safeguard officer mental health before and after mass casualty events

Laura Usher

Stefanie Friedhoff

Maj. Sam Cochran

Anand Pandya, MD

COPS
Community Oriented Policing Services
U.S. Department of Justice

Skyhorse Publishing

National Alliance on Mental Illness

As law enforcement executives it is our duty to keep our officers safe and healthy. Thank you to those that contributed to this important resource that helps us tackle the topics of resiliency as well as the effects of a mass casualty incident on officers' mental health both during and in the time that follows.

— Terrence Cunningham, Chief of Police, Wellesley (Massachusetts) Police Department and President of the International Association of Chiefs of Police

The mental health of our officers should be of the utmost importance. Whether issues are brought about by life circumstances, tragedy, critical incidents, or on-the-job stress, it is incumbent upon us as leaders to acknowledge the realness of the situation and to provide opportunities for help. As agency heads, we have the opportunity to provide permission to our agencies to speak openly and candidly about the mental health of our members.

— Colonel Matt Langer, Chief of Police, Minnesota State Patrol

This project was supported by cooperative agreement 2013-CK-WX-K038 awarded by the Office of Community Oriented Policing Services, U.S. Department of Justice. The opinions contained herein are those of the author(s) and do not necessarily represent the official position or policies of the U.S. Department of Justice. References to specific agencies, companies, products, or services should not be considered an endorsement by the author(s) or the U.S. Department of Justice. Rather, the references are illustrations to supplement discussion of the issues. The Internet references cited in this publication were valid as of the date of publication. Given that URLs and websites are in constant flux, neither the author(s) nor the COPS Office can vouch for their current validity.

Recommended citation:
Usher, Laura, Stefanie Friedhoff, Sam Cochran, and Anand Pandya. 2016. *Preparing for the Unimaginable: How Chiefs Can Safeguard Officer Mental Health Before and After Mass Casualty Events*. Washington, DC: Office of Community Oriented Policing Services.

Contents

Letter from the Director

Dear colleagues,

It's hard to imagine that an incident as horrific as those that occurred in Newtown, Charleston, and San Bernardino could occur in our own communities. Indeed, events of this kind are rare. But they do happen, and law enforcement leaders must be prepared not only for a possible incident but also for the aftermath that would follow.

Though most agencies have trained and equipped their officers for immediate response to mass casualties, few have prepared their personnel for the psychological fallout. Tragic events can have a profound effect on first responders, who may suffer emotional distress that lingers long afterward, leading to personal problems, alcoholism, post-traumatic stress disorder, and even suicide.

To help the Newtown (Connecticut) Police Department cope with the murder of 26 people, including 20 children, at Sandy Hook Elementary School, the COPS Office reached out to the National Alliance on Mental Illness (NAMI) to provide guidance. *Preparing for the Unimaginable* is the result of NAMI's work with Newtown's police chief, Michael Kehoe.

This unique publication offers expert advice and practical tips for helping officers to heal emotionally, managing public reaction, dealing with the media, building relationships with other first responder agencies, and much more. But what makes this handbook especially helpful are the case studies and stories from the field contributed by chiefs, officers, and mental health professionals who have lived through traumatic incidents.

We especially want to thank Chief Kehoe for his commitment to this effort, which required reliving a traumatic event. He and the other law enforcement professionals who contributed their personal experiences deserve our thanks for being open about this issue and sharing their lessons learned.

It is our hope that this handbook will be read by police chiefs and sheriffs throughout the country. Though *Preparing for the Unimaginable* focuses on mass casualty incidents, traumatic events arise in everyday police work as well, and their effect cannot be overstated.

The COPS Office is dedicated to promoting all aspects of officer wellness and safety, and as the *Final Report of the President's Task Force on 21st Century Policing* noted, the wellness and safety of law enforcement officers is critical not only to themselves, their colleagues, and their agencies but also to public safety. We applaud NAMI for bringing the critical issue of officer mental health to the forefront with this eye-opening publication.

Sincerely,

Ronald L. Davis
Director
Office of Community Oriented Policing Services

Foreword: Leadership When the Unimaginable Occurs

The Sandy Hook Elementary School shooting on December 14, 2012 caused a collective pause in the United States because of the brutality of the actions against the most vulnerable members of society. As the events unfolded and the world became aware of the devastation that occurred in an elementary school, police officers throughout the state of Connecticut were already busy handling a multitude of important responsibilities required when a tragedy befalls a community.

The ability of media to quickly share the news of tragic events adds to the stress and trauma normally associated with highly critical events. Law enforcement must initially respond to these events to mitigate the dangers inherent in the crisis. Then they must successfully navigate the aftermath, including daily intrusions and reminders of the tragedy from the media and offers of assistance from hundreds of well-intentioned community members and visitors arriving with stuffed animals, flowers, food, and other gifts.

In addition to responding to traumatic events, dealing with the scope and duration of the aftermath of tragedies is one of the most important concerns of police chiefs and sheriffs throughout the country.

Ensuring the mental wellness and health of first responders has long been an underappreciated task for the heads of police agencies. U.S. law enforcement has learned from tragic events over the years and now trains to respond to threats with the best equipment and practices known today. However, many chiefs are not prepared to deal effectively with the intense scope and unanticipated duration of the aftermath of these events, and many chiefs are unaware of the impact such events will have on their communities and the officers in their agencies.

The Sandy Hook Elementary School shooting was an unprecedented event in my career in law enforcement. Coping with the aftermath of the incident raised my awareness of how traumatic experiences affect the mental health and wellness of officers; thus, I asked the National Alliance on Mental Illness to work with me on developing this guide, which will provide chiefs and sheriffs with awareness and guidance on best practices for safeguarding the mental health and wellness of first responders in the early moments of critical events and during the long aftermath. This guide will also raise awareness for the many stressors associated with critical events.

As chiefs or sheriffs, we can make a difference in the quality of life our brave men and women will experience from hire to retire and beyond. Protecting the health and wellness of officers under our command is as important as any training an officer gets throughout his or her career. Our officers make many sacrifices during their careers, and their emotional well-being should be among our top priorities.

Michael Kehoe
Chief of Police (ret.), Newtown, Connecticut

Foreword: Mental Wellness Needs New Focus

The overwhelming probability is that you will not need this guide. The likelihood of a mass casualty event is so low that no law enforcement agency has been able to develop expertise in dealing with such incidents, let alone the traumatic psychological aftermath they have on first responders. But when these events do occur, they can have a wide-ranging impact on your agency and your officers. Should the unimaginable happen, having thought-through officer support will be invaluable. You can take action to prepare. The steps in this guide will benefit your agency even if you never experience a mass casualty event, because all officers are exposed to traumatic events throughout their careers.

The goal of this guide is to provide law enforcement executives with best practices regarding first responder mental health—best practices learned from colleagues unfortunate enough to have experienced a mass casualty event. The National Alliance on Mental Illness brought together chiefs, mental health professionals, and others with first-hand knowledge to provide readers with a concise compendium of what worked and what did not.

This guide is chronologically organized, beginning with pre-incident preparation and concluding with long-term aftercare. It provides chiefs and command staff with concrete tools to set up a mental health response structure now, when there is time. Trauma is an occupational hazard for first responders, yet officer mental health is a topic that often does not receive proper attention. It has become clear that psychological trauma is every bit as devastating as physical trauma, and the cumulative nature of these events can lead to post-traumatic stress disorder, alcoholism, divorce, depression, suicide, and other emotional problems that manifest years after the events occurred. This is why law enforcement agencies must explore long-term care.

First responder mental health needs new focus. Each year more and more officers suffer because they have not received proper psychological support. Officers are reluctant to request assistance for fear of being branded mentally weak or in the belief that seeking help will negatively impact their career. Administrators fail to provide this support because of a lack of understanding.

We hope that by sharing our experiences and lessons learned through this guide, we can contribute to a better understanding of officer wellness in the aftermath of these events and support other chiefs through a major challenge of leadership. We want to foster change in the way law enforcement agencies support officer wellness now, whether or not they ever experience a mass casualty event, and, ultimately, to help keep more good officers on the job.

John Edwards
Chief of Police, Oak Creek, Wisconsin

Marc Montminy
Chief of Police, Manchester, Connecticut

Michael Kehoe
Chief of Police (ret.), Newtown, Connecticut

Daniel Oates
Chief of Police, Miami Beach, Florida

Preface

On December 14, 2012, the Sandy Hook Elementary School shooting in Newtown, Connecticut—which left 26 dead, including 20 first-grade students—shocked the nation. It was one of the deadliest mass shootings in U.S. history, and the outpouring of support from people around the country and around the world was overwhelming. The Sandy Hook event reignited several debates: gun control, school safety, and the role of mental health services in ensuring public safety. While little has changed on these fronts, the lasting legacy of Sandy Hook may be the new light it shed on police officer mental health.

Many people would say that police officers have the strength and stoicism to bear a great deal more than the average citizen, and that is probably true. But any person who comes face to face with the horrors of a mass casualty event will be deeply affected, and many will need support to move past it. While they may be more resilient, law enforcement officers also quietly deal with an outsized share of our society's violence and death. As a result, too many officers struggle with alcoholism, post-traumatic stress disorder, and depression. It has become increasingly evident to police leaders that every officer deserves support to deal with the stresses and horrors that are part of the job.

In 2013, the U.S. Department of Justice's Office of Community Oriented Policing Services reached out to us at the National Alliance on Mental Illness (NAMI) to provide assistance to the Newtown Police Department. NAMI is the nation's largest grassroots mental health organization; we provide education, support, and advocacy to improve the lives of people living with mental health conditions and their families. We, along with our more than 900 local NAMI affiliates and state organizations in communities across the country, have a long history of partnering with law enforcement agencies to improve responses to community members in mental health crisis.

In Newtown, our charge was different: to support officer mental health. After meeting with Michael Kehoe, then chief of police in Newtown, as well as other community leaders, it became clear that this community had many mental health resources already available and a healthy skepticism about another offer of help from an outside organization unfamiliar with the community. Kehoe said if NAMI wanted to do something with a lasting impact, we should write a playbook for chiefs on how to safeguard officer mental health in the early days after a mass casualty event. He said that events like Sandy Hook rewrite the rules—for dealing with the media, for coordinating with other agencies, and for officer mental health. His hope was that other chiefs would benefit from the lessons he learned.

With Chief Kehoe's leadership, we convened an expert advisory group of police chiefs who had experienced mass casualty events in their communities, along with the mental health professionals who advised them, to gather lessons learned and guidance for other chiefs. After the expert advisory group meeting, we also sought guidance from numerous police leaders, mental health professionals, and trauma and media experts. Finally, we reviewed the research on what works to help people recover from trauma.

Mass casualty events, despite their frequency in the news, are relatively rare in the career of a police chief. With that in mind, the guidance offered in this publication should be understood as lessons learned combined with research about what has worked. Our recommendations are not gospel truth. Our hope is to contribute to the conversation about police officer wellness and to support chiefs who face these incidents in the future.

Acknowledgments

NAMI, the National Alliance on Mental Illness, is particularly grateful to the Office of Community Oriented Policing Services (COPS Office) for their support and guidance throughout this project. We particularly wish to thank Kimberly Nath, our project manager, for championing the cause of officer mental health and supporting us every step of the way. We also owe special thanks to retired Chief Michael Kehoe of Newtown, Connecticut, for his vision and leadership and to the other chiefs and mental health professionals who shared their time and expertise as part of NAMI's expert advisory group. This guide is possible only because of their willingness to share first-hand experiences.

The expert advisors included the following:

- **Michael Kehoe**, chief of police (ret.), Newtown, Connecticut, who oversaw the response to the Sandy Hook school shooting in 2012

- **John Edwards**, chief of police, Oak Creek, Wisconsin, who oversaw the response to the Sikh Temple of Wisconsin shooting in 2012

- **Marc Montminy**, chief of police, Manchester, Connecticut, who oversaw the response to the workplace shooting at Hartford Distributors in 2010

- **Daniel Oates**, chief of police, Miami Beach, Florida, who oversaw the response to the Aurora Century 16 Theater shooting in 2012 when he was chief of police in Aurora, Colorado

- **James Rascati**, licensed clinical social worker, whose company, Behavioral Health Consultants, LLC supported Chief Montminy after the Hartford Distributors shooting and Chief Kehoe after the Sandy Hook Elementary School shooting

- **John Nicoletti**, PhD, police psychologist, Nicoletti-Flater Associates, PLLP, who was involved in the responses to the Columbine High School shooting in 1999, the Aurora Century 16 Theater shooting in 2012, and several other mass casualty and active shooter incidents

We also thank the many law enforcement officers, medical and mental health professionals, colleagues, and friends who provided expertise, personal experience, and review of this guide:

James Baker, Director, Advocacy, International Association of Chiefs of Police

Amanda Burstein, Manager, Advocacy, International Association of Chiefs of Police

Ron Clark, RN, MS, APSO, Sergeant (ret.), Connecticut State Police; Chairman of the Board, Badge of Life

Kit Cummings, Lieutenant (ret.), Blacksburg (Virginia) Police Department; Law Enforcement Peer Specialist, Virginia Law Enforcement Assistance Program

AJ DeAndrea, Sergeant, Arvada (Colorado) Police Department

Mark DiBona, Patrol Sergeant, Seminole County (Florida) Sheriff's Department; Director, Badge of Life

Frank Dowling, MD, Clinical Associate Professor of Psychiatry, State University of New York (SUNY) at Stony Brook University; Medical Advisor, Police Organization Providing Peer Assistance

Ken Duckworth, MD, Medical Director, National Alliance on Mental Illness

Alexander Eastman, MD, MPH, FACS, Lieutenant and Deputy Medical Director, Dallas Police Department

Douglas Fuchs, Chief of Police, Redding (Connecticut) Police Department

Melissa Glaser, LPC, Community Outreach Coordinator, Newtown Recovery and Resiliency Team

Ingrid Herrera-Yee, PhD, Manager, Veterans, Military and Advocacy, National Alliance on Mental Illness

Ron Honberg, JD, Senior Policy Advisor, National Alliance on Mental Illness

Valerie Hunter, MA, LMFT, OTR, National Director, Organization Development and Talent Management, National Alliance on Mental Illness

Lori Kehoe, RN

Matt Langer, Colonel, Chief of the State Patrol, Minnesota

Gary MacNamara, Chief of Police, Fairfield (Connecticut) Police Department

Catherine Martin-Doto, PhD, Corporate Psychologist, Psychological Services, Toronto Police Service

Karen Meyer, Inspector, Ontario Provincial Police

Andy O'Hara, Sergeant (ret.), California Highway Patrol; Founder, Badge of Life

A.D. Paul, Sergeant, Plano (Texas) Police Department

Frank Petrullo, Director, Police Organization Providing Peer Assistance

Louise Pyers, Executive Director, Connecticut Alliance to Benefit Law Enforcement

Scott Ruszczyk, President, Newtown Police Officer's Union

C.J. Scallon, MPsy, Director, Critical Incident Stress Management / Peer Support Unit Sergeant, Norfolk (Virginia) Police Department; Vicarious Trauma Fellow, Northeastern University and the International Association of Chiefs of Police

John Violanti, PhD, Research Professor, Department of Epidemiology and Environmental Health, University of Buffalo

How to Read This Guide

This guide was written for law enforcement executives but with two different types of readers in mind. You may be interested because you want to build resiliency in your agency and prepare for a mass casualty event. In that case, you will have some time to read carefully and make a plan to ensure officer mental wellness is a priority. Alternatively, you may be reading this guide because a mass casualty event has occurred and you need guidance. You do not have time for in-depth discussion—you need to know what other chiefs recommend, and you need to know it fast.

To assist both types of readers, this guide offers nuanced explanations and narratives as well as quick facts, tip sheets, and summaries. We hope you can quickly find what you need via the detailed table of contents and the keyword index.

Trauma experts distinguish between the before, during, and after of a traumatic event. Where you are on this timeline, as an individual and as an agency, determines what information you need. That's why this guide is structured like a timeline.

> Where you are on this timeline, as an individual and as an agency, determines what information you need.

Chapters 1–4 deal with what you need to know to prepare to support officers before a mass casualty event. The only time you have to prepare for a mass casualty event is before one occurs. Thus, these chapters provide chiefs with the information they need to start building a more resilient force and preparing for a mass casualty event. Chapter 1 explains why officer mental wellness is important to any law enforcement agency and defines what we mean by psychological trauma and resiliency. Chapter 2 includes recommendations for building resiliency in your agency—these are valuable steps regardless of whether you ever experience a mass casualty event. Chapter 3 lays out specific steps for preparing for a mass casualty event, and chapter 4 discusses what you need to know about working with the media during a high-profile incident and how to prepare now.

Chapter 5 includes what you need to know during a mass casualty event. This is the most important chapter for chiefs in an immediate crisis. It offers fast and practical advice and helps everyone understand what is instantly needed during a mass casualty event.

Chapters 6–8 deal with the aftermath of a mass casualty event. These chapters deliver crucial details on the aftermath of a mass casualty event and will guide chiefs through the long struggle toward a new normal. These chapters identify new challenges that your community and your agency, your officers, and your leadership will face, as well as strategies for addressing those challenges. The chapters are laid out chronologically, but we did not attach specific time frames to each chapter because situations evolve differently in each community. Chapters 6–8 are also important for chiefs who are preparing their agencies for a mass casualty event and thus are interested in a fuller picture of the challenges they may face. While these chapters do not provide a comprehensive summary of every possible challenge that occurs after a mass casualty event, they do run the gamut from how to deal with outsiders visiting your community to how to resolve internal conflicts. Separating officer wellness from this array of issues is difficult because officers can feel traumatized by the incident, then stressed by the overwhelming workload, and then left behind if their command staff doesn't seem supportive.

The handout section at the end of this guide provides resources that we have assembled for various situations along the timeline. For example, you can distribute them now for educational purposes or use them to help support officers after a traumatic incident. They are meant to be copied, shared, and discussed.

In the end, officer mental wellness is not a subject that can be tackled in a few bullet points. We hope this comprehensive guide will allow you to access critical information from various angles, either piece by piece or in one complete read.

PART ONE.

Why Mental Wellness Matters

to You and Your Agency

1. Understanding Trauma and Resiliency

For many chiefs, the prospect of a mass shooting in your backyard is enough to start asking questions about officer mental wellness. The truth, however, is that day-to-day police work includes enough stress and exposure to trauma for chiefs to be concerned about every officer's mental wellness, whether or not you ever experience a mass casualty event. With that in mind, the following stories share some officers' experiences confronting and overcoming mental health concerns.

Stories from the field

The following stories are available in the handouts section in a photocopier-friendly format for distribution.

Chief John Edwards' story: Overcoming PTSD

John Edwards is the chief of police in Oak Creek, Wisconsin. He oversaw the police response to the 2012 shooting at the Sikh Temple of Wisconsin, where a white supremacist killed six worshippers and injured four others, including a police officer.

In 1989, I had been on the job for four years. One night, I was working the third shift when I came across an individual at a truck stop off the interstate. There was a car in a back area, where I would normally run into prostitutes, and I saw two people in the backseat.

When I saw the car, I felt something was wrong. They train us to trust the hairs on the back of our necks. I started to walk around the car, and I saw an Indiana plate. I knew immediately who it was. The FBI was looking for an escaped prisoner who had tried to shoot a sheriff's deputy in Indiana and taken a hostage before fleeing north with a prison employee who helped him escape.

As I was walking around the car, the driver got out of the backseat and came around the other side with two guns. He shouted, "Put your hands up! Get on the ground! Get on the ground!" Later on, when interviewed, he admitted that his plan was to get me on the ground, handcuff me, and then execute me.

I decided not to lie down on the ground. I had my hands raised, and I knew the gun would not penetrate my vest. I was young and agile, so I turned, put my head down, and ran. I knew I would get shot in the back. A bullet went through my jacket and my badge. Another hit me in the hand, which threw me off balance. I got behind a car, and I took my gun out to engage him. But he was already in the car, leaning out the open window and pointing his guns back in my direction. I was going to shoot him, but I saw two people just behind him at the gas station in the line of fire, so I ran to my car and chased him on the expressway, into the next county south.

He and his accomplice stopped at a farm and holed up in a barn. His accomplice was a psychiatrist, and she had medication on her. They both took medication and overdosed. When they were found, they were unconscious but alive.

When he went to trial, the jury found him guilty of reckless use of a weapon but not guilty of attempted murder. They said if he'd been trying to kill me, he would have hit me more than twice.

When these things happen, you either get angry, or you go into a shell. A doctor asked me later what I would have done if I had been able to stop them. I would have shot them both. That's not what you are supposed to do, but I was just so angry that they had tried to kill me.

> They said if he'd been trying to kill me, he would have hit me more than twice.

Right afterward, I was at the hospital. There was nothing life-threatening about my injuries, but it hit me that I almost died. I went back to the police department, and they interviewed me right away. Later, we found out that my interview was completely wrong. I swore that the woman's hair was white blonde, and it was actually black. I got tunnel vision and focused on the gun. I could probably still tell you the serial number on that gun, but I got all the other details wrong. Now I know that there's an adrenaline dump during these incidents, and a rest period is needed to remember correctly.

Afterward, I was treated like a hero. I got a letter of commendation and an award ceremony. That was really hard because I knew I screwed up. I approached the car wrong. I didn't see his hands. The whole time I was thinking, "Shit, this is wrong. This is wrong." But I still did it. The hero label is a pretty heavy burden to put on somebody who knows they made a mistake.

When I got back to work after two months of medical leave, the chief called me into his office. The chief was a World War II vet, and his whole office was a memorial to World War II. He said, "I always like to talk to someone who has tasted a bit of the lead. You hear about these doctors, but you don't need doctors. You just need to suck it up."

So I did. I sucked it up for about two years. I was paranoid on calls. I was hypersensitive. It got so bad that once an elderly man asked me to unlock his car for him, and I made him stand 50 feet away.

I couldn't sleep. Once, my wife moved in her sleep, and I jumped up on top of her and grabbed her by the throat.

When a new chief came in, I decided I couldn't take it anymore. I told him I needed help, that I had to go see someone. He took my gun and badge away for seven months. He said he wasn't letting anyone get a disability on his watch. I had just gotten married, and my wife was pregnant.

I went to several doctors, and they all said, "This guy isn't lying. He does have PTSD," but that wasn't enough for the chief. PTSD wasn't as well known back then. The mayor got wind of what the chief had done and intervened. I was finally able to get my job back and get reimbursed for all that time.

More than 20 years later, the Sikh Temple shooting brought back my PTSD. It was about two or three days after the shooting, and I went to the hospital to see Lieutenant Brian Murphy, the officer who was shot during the incident. His wife was sitting next to him in the hospital room. He couldn't communicate, so I took her out into the hallway and tried to explain the disability benefits to her. A few nights later, I woke up at 3 a.m., and my bed was soaked. I was sweating profusely, crying uncontrollably, shaking, and trembling, just like after my shooting. The scene of Brian in the hospital bed is what brought it all back. It was a snapshot of many years before when I was in the hospital after my shooting, my wife was in the chair next to me, and my sergeant came in to talk to me and my wife.

When I came into work, I called my captains into my office, and I broke down. I told them, "You cannot tell the officers; the supervisors can't know." But I wanted the captains to know so they could watch out for me.

The Milwaukee area has police officer support teams to assist officers after a critical incident. I called in a lieutenant from Milwaukee to come to one of my staff meetings and talk with the supervisors about what they were feeling. The room was very quiet. At that point, I felt that I had to tell them what had happened to me. I told them that I didn't want them to have to deal with that. It was important for them to know it's okay if it happens, and don't suck it up.

I went to see a psychologist who works with us at the police department. I spent about three hours talking, getting a tune-up. It reassured me and got me back on track.

One of the things I'm doing now is trying to create a branch of the city employee assistance provider (EAP) to provide six visits to a psychologist or psychiatrist for police- and fire-related PTSD. The city pays for it, but they don't look at the medical records. This is not part of the disability determination process, and we control the network of doctors, so we know that officers can't use it to game the system. The goal is that early intervention can make it not as severe as it was for me and can prevent worker's comp claims down the line.

Lori Kehoe's story: The impact of trauma on law enforcement spouses

Lori Kehoe, RN, is a former hospice nurse and advocate for her adult son with special needs. She is also the wife of Michael Kehoe, the retired chief of police who oversaw the law enforcement response to the 2012 Sandy Hook school shooting in Newtown, Connecticut.

December 14, 2012, the day of the Sandy Hook school shooting, was very long. I did not expect Mike to come home that night. After all, they had cots at the police department; they had uniforms and showers. When he did arrive home at midnight, he talked and talked until he passed out in the middle of a sentence. At 6:00 a.m., he was out the door. I offered to answer phones or e-mail. His answer was "no,

I got it covered." I offered to make him breakfast, and the answer—which became a common phrase in our home—was "no, I got it covered." It was rare that he needed me for anything.

This became the schedule: 6:00 a.m. to midnight. Mike was not available to talk on the phone, so our time was from midnight to two in the morning, when he would talk and tell me every little detail of the day. Each night it was necessary for Mike to decompress, and I saw it as my job to be available and to listen and do whatever he needed. He would continue to literally fall asleep talking. When Mike started yelling in his sleep, I could tell he was reliving the incident. This schedule lasted for about four months, and it became extremely isolating.

Many family and friends were supportive, but a lot of people couldn't deal with the trauma. They would break down crying on the phone. Or people were afraid to call because they didn't want to intrude. And the last thing you want to do when something dramatic like this happens is dump it all on someone who can't handle it. I relied on the people who called me to be my support system, because I didn't dare reach out. I was isolated but, at the same time, saturated with the media. Newtown was on the news for three or four days straight. You couldn't turn on the TV without seeing it.

Mike does not get upset. He is always cool, calm, and collected. He doesn't bounce off the walls. A few weeks after the shooting, he came home and was pacing and absolutely agitated beyond agitated. He was concerned about his officers committing suicide. He expressed his concerns, and we came up with options for him to execute the next day. I was always the sounding board, bringing whatever common sense I could muster to the table.

> Recognizing those stages [of grief] allowed me to give
> Mike all the room he needed and understand
> the changes that were happening.

Those were the days when I would wonder, whom do you call for answers? After all, isn't there always someone to call for help in life? When you got a flat tire, you call your dad. If your cake won't rise, you call your mom. I realized there is *no one* to call when 20 children get blown away in your town. You're watching your partner struggle with all these questions and no answers.

After 20 years as a hospice nurse, I understand grief and crisis. Without that experience, we probably wouldn't still be married. Understanding the process of grief, I was able to identify a little anger this week, depression the next, bargaining, denial. Recognizing those stages allowed me to give Mike all the room he needed and understand the changes that were happening.

He was suddenly in control of everything. All of a sudden, he was telling me what to do and when. It was bizarre from a man who never gave orders at home. Then I realized he needed to be in control, to maintain order. He was spending his days making rapid-fire decisions continuously for weeks on end.

I went to the police department the day after the event. When I got off the highway, life changed. There was an officer and his town car on every corner for the entire length of the town—hundreds of officers in a little quaint country one-horse town, where they usually had no more than five officers on a shift. The police department was inundated with flowers, food, and gifts—so much that they almost couldn't do their jobs. Then I knew why he had everything covered: I suppose if you had 5,000 cops at your beck and call, you'd have it covered too.

Finally in August (nine months after the shooting), Mike came home and said, "I got to something on my desk today that was on my desk before December 14." I thought to myself, "It's August, and the trauma is finally over."

A year after the shooting, I was mentally and emotionally not functioning, almost to the point of not getting out of bed. And even though I'm a nurse, I didn't know about trauma—I didn't know what trauma could do to a person or that there was such a thing as PTSD by association. I was so angry. I was mad at everyone and everything. I was depressed beyond belief, alone, and isolated.

The first anniversary was a turning point. The media stayed away, and I realized it was going to start simmering down. I realized it was not my job to take care of Mike any longer. So I went online and googled "law enforcement spouses and trauma," and I found a treatment center called the West Coast Post-Trauma Retreat in California. They had a week-long spouses' treatment program a couple of times a year.

I called them expecting them to turn me down because Newtown was such a large incident—I didn't want my trauma to overshadow someone else's. Instead, they interviewed me on the phone and said, "It sounds like you could use our help. Come on out." They taught me that the trauma actually changes your brain—you can see it on an MRI. In addition to five full days of intervention and counseling, they did a physical treatment on me called eye movement desensitization and reprocessing (EMDR). It's designed to reduce the emotion that goes with the thoughts about the traumatic experience. It was extremely effective.

The treatment was necessary, and it changed my life. I absolutely came back a new woman, and I got better and better after treatment. Today, we're good.

I think education is so important. If an incident like this affects the officer, it affects the family. They may never talk about it, but it's still happening. And in some ways, I was lucky—many people react to trauma with alcohol abuse and out of control behavior that creates chaos. That did not happen to my officer.

You need to know that when a trauma occurs, alcohol abuse, depression, and chaotic behaviors can be symptoms of PTSD. Whether it is the officer or the family member displaying symptoms, you need to know what it looks like and that it is a physical injury. There is treatment. You can and must do something about it.

Sergeant Andy O'Hara's story: Managing cumulative PTSD and helping to prevent officer suicide

Andy O'Hara is a retired California Highway Patrol officer and the founder of The Badge of Life, an organization of active and retired law enforcement officers dedicated to preventing officer suicide.

Rather than coming from one incident, my PTSD was cumulative. I compare all the things that happen on a regular basis in police work to bee stings: One is tolerable, but as they build up, the pain becomes overwhelming.

In the course of my career with the California Highway Patrol, I accumulated 24 years of traumatic experiences—11 years as a sergeant and the rest as a traffic officer. I spent most of my career on the road, so I saw accidents on a daily basis. Some were gruesome: decapitations and dismemberments. I heard a lot of screams, and honestly you become tired of them. I responded to murders and suicides, backing up our local police departments. I saw injured and abused children. I was assaulted.

Probably the biggest incident that finally triggered a full blown case of PTSD was when an officer of mine was killed. He wanted to work overtime, and I knew he was tired. He pleaded with me to work, and I didn't want him to, but I relented and let him. He fell asleep on his motorcycle. I responded to the scene and half of his head was missing.

> In police work, the opportunity for mistakes is pretty high, and they haunt you.

Cumulative PTSD can be difficult to treat because you've got so much to deal with. You get into feelings like guilt and self-blame. You've got mistakes—dirty little secrets and mistakes in judgment. Everybody makes mistakes. In police work, the opportunity for mistakes is pretty high, and they haunt you. You take a lot of responsibility for things that happen on the road. Officers think about how they might have prevented it, how they might have gotten there sooner. All the "what ifs" will kill you.

It all begins to compile and becomes a big bundle of yuck that catches up to you in nightmares, depression, and flashbacks.

After my officer died, I took the blame for it. I couldn't forgive myself. I went through crying spells. My temper flared at home and at work. It became explosive. I started having panic attacks and anxiety. I started withdrawing. I became almost agoraphobic. The flashbacks reached a point where I couldn't sleep. I tried alcohol as a coping technique, and it worked: I could sleep.

I was a closet drinker. At first, I always quit 8 to 10 hours before work, but eventually I became an alcoholic. I was starting to show up to work with the odor of alcohol on my breath. Ultimately, drinking just made it worse; I wasn't able to suppress the feelings with the alcohol.

I started to get scared of losing my career. And there was pressure from my wife. I knew I had to quit drinking, and when I did I felt worse because I didn't have the sedative effects of the alcohol to overcome the flashbacks and anxiety.

About a year later, I became suicidal and went into the hospital. I've been on meds and in therapy since then, and I eventually retired on disability.

I've been able to manage my problems. You don't cure PTSD; you learn to manage it. I've been able to manage the depression, the flashbacks, and the problems sleeping. But I still get panic attacks and anxiety, especially in traffic and in crowds. I don't handle stress very well. When I was on patrol, I was the figure of calm; nothing could bother me. Today, even driving is a challenge for me.

After I had gone through a lot of recovery, I reflected back on things that I could have done to avoid the predicament I got into. It never occurred to me to get into therapy during my career; I had never even heard of therapy. But it works pretty well. If I had gotten therapy back then, I might not have had to retire.

I got to thinking about why officers don't try therapy or medication. There are officers suffering from anxiety and PTSD, and they are determined to suffer through it for the rest of their lives. I think in this day and age, when officers are being questioned on a lot of things (shootings, arrests, and brutality), a lot of that could be avoided through some good therapy. And I think people are scared of medication. Medication doesn't necessarily affect your ability to work, but officers don't know that.

Sergeant Mark DiBona's story: Using his personal struggles to help other cops

Mark DiBona is a deputy sheriff with the Seminole County Sheriff's Department in central Florida and is on the board of directors for The Badge of Life.

It was my lifelong dream to be a cop, and I started on the job at age 21. I've been in law enforcement for 30 years and a supervisor for 17.

About eight years ago, I was going through some tough times at work. I wasn't getting along with my immediate supervisor. We were both alpha males, but we had completely different styles of working and supervision. He was hard headed and strict, and I tried to be approachable to my guys. I felt he was very disrespectful. We became argumentative, insulting each other. He told me I wasn't aggressive enough, that I had to be harder on my guys. I took things to heart. He gave me an evaluation of "below standards." I felt worthless, like maybe he was right, maybe this job wasn't for me anymore. I felt like I couldn't do anything right.

This went on for a few months. It affected me physically. I gained 40 pounds. I refused to shave. I started coming in with my uniform wrinkled. I didn't go to my wife for help. I thought, "If you aren't a cop, you don't understand." The stigma is if you show a weakness, if you say something's bothering you, they look at you like you are weak.

So all this is already happening, and one night I am at the fire station, and a woman pulls up in her car. She cried, "My baby isn't breathing!" Just before she pulled up, the firemen had gone out on a call, so I did CPR on the baby. It seemed like I did CPR for an hour.

The baby died. I went to the funeral and the wake. I started to get nightmares about him, like maybe I could have done better. I can still feel that baby in my arms.

I told my boss, and he said, "You were just doing your job," like it wasn't a big deal.

I started feeling more worthless. I had lots of nightmares, waking up in cold sweats. I started thinking about the baby that died, and all the other stuff came up too: the horrible crashes I've seen, the victims of sexual abuse, the victims of robbery, the bad guys, the friends who died in the line of duty. I thought, "I don't want to be a cop anymore because this line of work sucks." One night, it hit me: This job is not for me; I'm failing really fast. I tried to fight the thoughts, but I felt like I was drowning. I attempted suicide twice that night.

I got lucky. A car pulled up, and it was another cop. He talked me down. I went home because I couldn't go back to work that night. I was afraid of losing my job. I thought they would take away my gun and put me in the hospital.

I was diagnosed with PTSD and depression. I'm on medication, and it's helped me to focus. I was concerned about the meds; could I still be a cop? But I can; it's not a problem whatsoever. I'm still an active deputy sheriff.

I called a close friend in Boston. He said he wanted me to come up there to get help. I went to Massachusetts and got some therapy, and then I went back to Florida a week and half later. I bounced back and forth between therapists. It wasn't clicking because the therapist didn't have any police background. I didn't go to the employee assistance provider because they are countywide, not specialized to police. I just wasn't in my comfort zone.

It was a difficult time in my life. I saw a person in me that I'd never seen before. There's that Michael Jackson song, "The Man in the Mirror." When I looked in the mirror, I didn't like the guy I saw. I didn't like his looks; I didn't like him. I felt weak. I knew in my heart that something was wrong, but it was hard to accept when I was diagnosed.

I stopped going to therapy, and I started looking on online. I found fascinating articles about police mental health, suicide, stigma, and an organization called The Badge of Life. I never realized that support was out there. I had a friend, a fellow officer, who committed suicide, but I thought it was just a family problem.

I started to go to a support group in central Florida, just cops talking to cops. I found a therapist who is a retired cop. During the course of all this, I got my marriage back on track. I felt guilty about the way I treated my wife, and I apologized. She had felt helpless. She was trying to get me help, and I wouldn't take the help.

I was diagnosed with PTSD and depression. I'm on medication, and it's helped me to focus. I was concerned about the meds; could I still be a cop? But I can; it's not a problem whatsoever. I'm still an active deputy sheriff.

I've never had a suicidal thought since. I still have the nightmares, just not as much as I used to. I just feel a lot better now. I lost the weight I gained. I don't let it ruin my everyday life, ruin my job, ruin my marriage. On the days when I feel down, I've learned to control that—the anxiety, depression, and PTSD.

The biggest problem I have now is the stigma. When I'm open about it, the guys look at me funny. But there are others; when they hear my story, they come up to me and say, "Can I talk to you for a second?" There's nothing better than helping another cop through the issues that I experienced.

I really enjoy my life now, when for years I didn't. I still love being a cop.

Police officers aren't immune to trauma

For police officers, traumatic experiences are an occupational hazard: responding to car accidents, homicides, child abuse, domestic violence, and similarly negative events are part of the job. Law enforcement culture values self-reliance, stoicism, and strength. Officers, the thinking goes, can "suck it up" and continue working, so it is easy to assume that officers who are fit for duty are, by nature, resilient.

However, resilience can be a matter of degree, and not all traumatic events are created equal. For example, most people are resilient enough to read about the death of someone they did not know without becoming overwhelmed by anxiety. But when they read about the death of a friend, they react more strongly. Similarly, most police officers may be able to tolerate a more vivid exposure to death or violence than the general public, but there are situations, such as mass casualty events, where the traumatic stress simply exceeds an officer's ability to cope without support.

> "Rather than coming from one incident, my PTSD was cumulative. I compare all the things that happen on a regular basis in police work to bee stings: One is tolerable, but as they build up, the pain becomes overwhelming."
>
> — *Sergeant Andy O'Hara (ret.), California Highway Patrol*

> **Defining psychological trauma**
>
> *Psychological trauma* is what we call a person's emotional response to an extremely negative experience, such as suffering life-threatening danger, injury, or abuse; witnessing the death of others; or losing a colleague in the line of duty. Experiencing a traumatic incident does not mean someone is damaged or doomed to develop post-traumatic stress disorder (PTSD). Such an experience simply means that the event occurred, is now part of a person's sensory memory, and needs to be processed and integrated.

Officers can also experience *cumulative trauma.* As they encounter death, injury, and dangerous situations with some regularity, the impact of these experiences can accumulate over time. These events do not make an officer tougher. Rather, research shows that the more traumatic incidents someone experiences over the course of a lifetime, the more likely another event may tip the balance. Even officers known to be resilient may find recovery harder after yet another incident or after a particularly stressful incident.

In an environment where frequent exposure to trauma is part of the job, recognizing the consequences of cumulative trauma can be particularly challenging. You may think an officer is resilient because he shows up at work every day but not know that he drinks every night to fall asleep. Similarly, an officer might be struggling with marital problems or suicidal thoughts and not recognize that the roots of those problems may lie at work and can be addressed with psychological support.

Another challenge to understanding the impact of trauma is that reactions can change over time. An officer who seems to be doing well may suddenly begin to struggle months or years later when confronted with an unwelcome reminder of the event. Or an officer may gradually become depressed and not recognize that the depression relates to the traumatic event.

To understand what fosters resilience and what types of support officers need after a traumatic event, we need to first take a closer look at how our brains and bodies respond to traumatic events.

The immediate impact of traumatic events

Most human beings have a similar biological response to a traumatic encounter. When we fear for our lives or experience another traumatic situation, adrenaline floods our bodies, making us more vigilant and helping us to survive. Everyone, no matter how experienced or disciplined, experiences this fight-or-flight response, during which all nonessential systems in the body shut down so energy can be directed toward the systems needed to either fight or flee.

This response affects our bodies in several ways:

- Shaking, especially of the hands. Not enough blood and oxygen is going to the small muscles in the body, impairing their ability to function normally.

- Stomach butterflies. The overall shutdown of all nonessential systems includes the digestive system. Throughout the day, the digestive tract constantly moves and contracts. When this stops, it creates the sensation of butterflies or knots.

- Tunnel vision. The visual field narrows. Officers often express concern that they did not see certain aspects of a scene (e.g., a pedestrian walking by or a car driving by); however, they cannot control this physiological response. During a fight-or-flight experience, if you choose to fight, you generally need to focus only on the object that poses the biggest risk (a gun, a knife, etc.). If you choose flight, you need to see only the escape route. Tunnel vision focuses your attention on your maximum chance of survival.

- Tunnel hearing. As with tunnel vision, the brain focuses only on the sounds it perceives as essential for survival and filters out anything extraneous. For example, officers may not hear someone shouting at them, or some shouts may sound muffled to officers during a fight-or-flight situation.

- Amnesia. Research suggests that high levels of stress can negatively impact memory, particularly short-term memory for simple facts. When faced with fight-or-flight decisions, the brain is concerned with survival, not detail. For example, law enforcement investigators might ask officers how many rounds they fired from their weapon during a critical incident, but some officers may not know because the brain was not concerned with bullet count; the brain was concerned with stopping the threat.

"[After the shooting,] I went back to the police department, and they interviewed me right away. Later, we found out that my interview was completely wrong. I swore that the woman's hair was white blonde, and it was actually black. I got tunnel vision and focused on the gun. I could probably still tell you the serial number on that gun, but I got all the other details wrong."

— *John Edwards, Chief of Police, Oak Creek, Wisconsin*

Once our safety and the safety of others are ensured, we try to regain a sense of normalcy over time. Our common biological reactions turn into more complex, individual coping mechanisms. Many people experience nightmares, anxiety, numbness, or anger—the range of normal reactions is wide. While these responses to a traumatic event can be upsetting or unexpected, that does not necessarily mean they are unusual or a sign of a persistent mental health problem. However, just because officers may be having a normal reaction to a traumatic event does not mean they shouldn't have support to deal with their response; in fact, support from the agency, from family and friends, and from mental health professionals can help officers return to the baseline of normal functioning more quickly.

It's important to note that having a strong reaction to a traumatic event is not a sign of weakness. The slight differences in how officers can experience a particular event, such as how close they were to the victims or how long they spent at the scene, can influence the intensity of their individual responses. Even with identical exposures to a traumatic event, officers' responses will differ based on factors like how they cope with stress, availability of social supports, prior trauma experience, and the overall stress in their lives.

The long-term impact of trauma

Everyone has their own timeline for healing from a traumatic incident. It is hard to predict who will improve and who will struggle. Most people recover after a traumatic incident, but some can develop more persistent or serious mental health conditions. This is not a sign of weakness or lack of willpower.

Serious problems can include depression, anxiety, post-traumatic stress disorder (PTSD), alcoholism, marital problems, or thoughts of suicide. If they arise, mental health conditions are generally not diagnosed until months and sometimes years after the traumatic experience. One reason for this delay in diagnosis is that many people react strongly to traumatic situations but recover on their own in a matter of weeks or months. For others, the symptoms and challenges may not be obvious, they may not understand that they are dealing with the effects of trauma, or they may not be willing to seek help. Sometimes people experience a delayed reaction: Someone who seemed fine may have a strong reaction at the anniversary of the event or when there's an unavoidable reminder, like the trial of the perpetrator.

Not all serious outcomes can be prevented, but many people can be helped and return to normal life even after a serious mental health problem; the sooner support is available, the better. Many long-term negative outcomes can be mitigated or prevented by building a resilient agency, promoting healthy coping strategies, and providing proactive support from a mental health professional.

Unresolved trauma is an officer safety issue

In addition to its personal impact on officers, unaddressed trauma can create an officer safety and work performance issue.

A lot has been learned in recent years about how military service can traumatize soldiers. Soldiers with PTSD can become counterproductive on duty and even destructive once back in their normal lives, for example by becoming a threat to themselves and their families. Suicide and domestic violence rates are high among veterans of recent wars.

While much less studied, police officers straddle a similar divide between life on and off duty. While doing their jobs, they may see the dark side of humanity in all its unimaginable forms and need their normal stress response to stay alive. Then they go off shift and are expected to switch off that reaction. Because that is not always possible, suicide, alcoholism and similar unhealthy coping mechanisms can be a problem for law enforcement officers.[1]

Unresolved trauma can negatively affect behavior both at work and at home. If an officer suffers from undetected PTSD, for example, he might be hypervigilant on the job, just as Chief Edwards describes in his story from the field (quoted on page 3). Hypervigilance is an important part of the trauma response as it helps us focus on the most essential information in a life-threatening situation. But when a threat has passed, hypervigilance can lead to behavior that is at best inappropriate and at worst unsafe (such as when a hypervigilant officer perceives a threat where others do not and shoots too soon).

Officers can also exhibit unsafe or unusual behavior when exposed to a trauma trigger. In a traumatic situation, our brain carefully registers all information coming in from the senses: What we smell, see, hear, taste, and touch when we are under maximum stress will be stored together with the biochemical equivalent of a massive warning sign. If an officer noticed a distinct smell during a traumatic incident, encountering the same smell months later can send him immediately back into survival mode. Officers need to understand and anticipate potential triggers to be confident and safe.

"There are officers suffering from anxiety and PTSD and they are determined to suffer through it for the rest of their lives. I think in this day and age, where officers are being questioned on a lot of things-- shootings, arrests, brutality—a lot of that could be avoided through some good therapy."

— *Sergeant Andy O'Hara (ret.), California Highway Patrol*

---

[1] Robert Kroll, "Managing the Dark Side: Treating Officers with Addiction," *The Police Chief* 81, no. 9 (September 2014), http://www.policechiefmagazine.org/magazine/index.cfm?fuseaction=display_arch&article_id=3492&issue_id=92014#2.

Avoidance is another common coping mechanism in the aftermath of trauma that can backfire if it does not recede: Some officers, often to their own surprise, may not react to a threat as readily as they used to because they are instinctively avoiding additional stress. Some officers may avoid situations that remind them of a traumatic event—a survivor of a car accident may avoid highways, for example.

These and other aspects of unresolved trauma also carry into officers' private lives and can make relationships complicated. In one recent study, for example, law enforcement officers with PTSD were four times more likely than those without PTSD to use physical violence in an intimate relationship; those with an alcohol dependency were eight times more likely than those who were not dependent on alcohol to physically attack a partner.[2]

Acknowledging that no one is immune to the impact of trauma allows chiefs to take a fresh look at some well-known challenges around officer mental health in law enforcement agencies. Providing adequate mental health services for officers can help them process a traumatic event and improve their performance. It's not just the right thing to do—it is essential to maintaining a healthy and strong force.

"In order to deliver professional, compassionate, and respectful policing services to the community, it makes sense that we take care of our own mental health and well-being, too—before you can take care of others you have to take care of yourself. So it is vital that officers have the support, tools, and education to ensure healthy interactions."

— *Inspector Karen Meyer, Wellness Unit Manager, Ontario Provincial Police*

Psychological resilience

It's important to know that after trauma, individuals cannot and probably should not go back to being the exact same people they were before. They grow and learn. They remember and think differently. They have moments when they are overcome by the stress but also moments of hope and optimism. This is psychological resilience, which simply means that a person who has had a traumatic experience is able to adapt and move past that experience over time.

People used to think that we are all born with different degrees of resilience and there's no way to change the baseline—people are either resilient or they are not.

---

[2] Karen Oehme et al., "Alcohol Abuse, PTSD, and Officer-Committed Domestic Violence," *Policing* 6, no.4 (2012), 418–430, http://policing.oxfordjournals.org/content/6/4/418.abstract.

> **Defining psychological resilience**
>
> *Psychological resilience* is an individual's or a community's ability to recover after a traumatic event. Resilience is not about being unaffected by negative emotions—almost everyone has negative feelings after a traumatic experience. Instead, resilience is the process that helps us balance negative emotions with positive ones and choose coping strategies that enable a gradual recovery. Someone who is resilient will react to a trauma in ways that reduce the risk of long-term problems.

Today, we know that resilience is more fluid than that. It is better to think of resilience as a process rather than just a trait. While some factors that can increase resiliency—such as having a sense of humor or having strong religious or spiritual beliefs—are not easily changed after someone has been traumatized, the right support systems can help most people recover successfully and prevent mental health problems in the future.

Support can come from work or personal life. Research suggests that people are more resilient when they feel that they are part of a cohesive and supportive group, including in the workplace. In a resilient agency officers are able to support each other, and they know that agency leaders care about their well-being. Everyone from the top down in your agency needs to know one another, have one another's backs, and support one another in difficult times.

At home, resilience is strengthened by emotional literacy (identifying and understanding our emotional reactions). It is also strengthened by a supportive family and friends and use of healthy strategies for coping with stress, like healthy eating, exercise, and sleep habits and taking time off to wind down from work.

Sometimes work stress is compounded by other factors that reduce resilience. For example, going through a divorce or losing a loved one can make it harder to recover from a traumatic event at work. Other risk factors include a personal or family history of depression, unhealthy eating or sleep habits, or the lack of access to a supportive group of friends.

Do we need to change law enforcement culture to promote resilience?

Given this information about trauma and resilience, chiefs may be unsure how to safeguard officer mental wellness especially after a mass casualty event. Looking back at their experiences, chiefs involved in mass casualty events realized that they had to do more than find the right mental health professionals and put in place the right supports: They also had to remove the taboo around talking about mental health and wellness.

Law enforcement culture often discourages officers from discussing mental health problems or from seeking help. Officers often feel their jobs or reputations are at stake if they admit to any vulnerability. Instead of reaching out for help, an officer who is struggling may turn to unhealthy coping mechanisms such as drinking, aggression, overwork, or even extreme exercising—and that's the case under normal conditions, not in the extraordinary circumstance of a mass casualty event.

Instead of these unhealthy coping mechanisms, officers need to feel free to make decisions to care for themselves, such as taking a day off or talking to a mental health professional. Officers may also need support to manage stress in healthy ways—like connecting with friends and family, moderate exercise, getting enough sleep, and eating well.

This is not about touchy-feely conversations; it's about supporting officers' mental health in the same way as you would their physical health and creating an agency culture that keeps officers resilient, adaptable, and fit for duty.

"I don't think we need to change the culture. The culture is what allows a cop to go toward the sound of gunfire and stop a threat. A cop's got to walk with a little bit of a swagger. We need to understand the culture better. There are things that need to change a little bit—like thinking we are Superman, that these things don't hurt us. Those are weaknesses in the culture, and we need to deal with them."

— *Sergeant AJ DeAndrea, Patrol Officer, Arvada, Colorado*

"When I got back to work after two months of medical leave, the chief called me into his office. The chief was a World War II vet and his whole office was a memorial to World War II. He said, 'I always like to talk to someone who has tasted a bit of the lead. You hear about these doctors, but you don't need doctors. You just need to suck it up.' "

— *John Edwards, Chief of Police, Oak Creek, Wisconsin*

Emotional literacy at a glance

Police officers are exposed to a significant amount of stress. Stress can be energizing or debilitating, and it affects both our physical and emotional well-being. Learning how to recognize and deal with stress takes education and practice, like any other skill. Preparation pays off, especially in a crisis.

Officers are trained to restrain their emotions. It's what makes it possible to do this challenging work. So, why should you talk about emotions? Because this kind of education—being able to recognize, understand, and describe emotions—helps us better cope with stress. Fortunately, you can understand your emotions without getting lost in them.

This is called *emotional literacy*: Learning about our emotional responses the same way we learn the alphabet and then beginning to read, understand, and act with better information at hand. For example, by knowing how the body responds to stress—adrenaline kicking in, leading to shaking hands, tunnel vision, and other symptoms—we can "read" our own responses during an incident and avoid confusion about why we react a certain way.

Emotional literacy allows us to recognize when stress begins to negatively affect us. Instead of feeling lost in guilt or shame in the aftermath of a critical incident, for example, we can recognize these are normal reactions to trauma and ask for help in dealing with them.

In short, emotional literacy can help police officers take charge of the mental challenges of police work and keep a clear mind to make safe decisions, maintain healthy relationships, and stay strong on the job.

PART TWO.

Preparing for a

Mass Casualty Event

2. Recommendations for Enhancing Resilience in Your Agency *Today*

While it may seem daunting to plan for a mass casualty event—something unprecedented for most law enforcement agencies—there are steps you can take now to prepare for the possibility. And the good news is that these steps will benefit your agency even if you never experience a mass casualty event. Starting now is key. After an incident, it will be hard to put together a strong mental health plan in the face of many other competing responsibilities.

To get you started, we have outlined steps you can take to address officer mental health in your agency. These steps are suggestions based on the experience of a small group of chiefs who have lived through mass casualty events, as well as current research on mental health and trauma. There will not be a perfect formula that will work for every agency, and your needs and resources may vary. But we hope these steps provide useful, concrete ways for you to start building robust officer wellness programs and a more resilient agency.

Take a personal interest in officer wellness

Officers take their cues from the command staff and supervisors, who take their cues from the chief. A great mental health support program means little if officers don't see their leaders take a personal interest. Here are some suggestions for how to show that officer wellness is a priority for you:

- **Assign someone as your representative on mental health issues, and make is clear this individual has your full support.** Later in this guide, we outline a role for a mental health incident commander to address these needs. You may not be able to be available personally to support all your officers, so make it clear that on mental health matters, the mental health incident commander is your representative.

- **Be present and visible for officers after a critical incident.** After a traumatic incident, officers will look at your reaction to decide whether the agency is taking their well-being seriously. Checking in personally with officers who were involved in a critical incident—and asking how they are and what you can do to help—will go a long way.

- **Be supportive and available every day.** You can do this by showing up at roll call and having an open door policy. If your agency is too large for you to make personal contact with all your officers regularly, set the example with your command staff and supervisors and direct them to look out for their reports.

- **Show officers that you value their work.** Employees who feel valued are less likely than those who do not to be stressed in their everyday work and more likely to report good mental health. Recognition of good work along with open and honest communication can help.

- **Proactively resolve conflict.** A mass casualty event will not unify your agency. Quite the opposite: the stress of a mass casualty event often worsens existing tensions or leads to new conflict. It's important to proactively address these conflicts and demonstrate to your officers that you take their concerns seriously.

- **Look for ways to build agency unity.** Officers' best support comes from one another. Look for ways to promote socializing and support, such as family night, kids' academies, an agency sports league, or other regular social events.

- **Share some of your personal reactions.** After a critical incident, it is okay for you to share some of your genuine emotional response with officers. If something affects you deeply, it's likely your officers are experiencing the same thing. Your willingness to share will make it easier for them to talk about it. If you seek out mental health support after a critical incident, tell your officers you have done so.

- **Set a healthy example.** When you need a day off, take one—and grant that same flexibility to your staff. When your officers are in fitness or mental health training, make an appearance and tell them something you are doing to ensure you stay healthy and resilient.

"When it's all said and done, no matter how big, bad, and tough we think we are, we need to pay attention to the issue of mental health. It comes down to relationships—understanding each other on an emotional level and taking care of each other. As a supervisor, I take seriously my responsibility for taking care of the guys."

— *Sergeant AJ DeAndrea, Patrol Officer, Arvada, Colorado*

Form a work group to recommend officer wellness programs and education

While it might seem more expedient to implement an array of officer wellness programs right away, a work group serves several purposes. First, it creates a forum for discussing wellness issues within the agency, which is an important step to helping officers feel comfortable with the change. Second, you will help ensure officer wellness programs are inviting for officers and take advantage of the mental health resources available in your community. Finally, by working *with* your labor force, you will help ensure that if there is a mass casualty event, it doesn't spark a conflict between labor and management over the availability of mental health services.

The work group should include command staff, supervisors, union leadership, mental health providers affiliated with the agency, and mental health providers from the broader community. It should be tasked with

- networking with mental health providers;

- assessing what sort of wellness education officers need;

- making recommendations about ongoing officer wellness programs;

- making recommendations about changes to policy related to psychological services after critical incidents (see "Review your psychological services policies and procedures" on page 30).

There is a lot of innovation in officer wellness programming. There are a variety of options, and your work group can help you narrow down which approaches match your agency's needs and resources. The work group may suggest implementing programs such as the following:

- **Presentations from officers who have experienced mental health challenges.** Fellow officers who have experienced and gotten through mental health challenges can help officers understand that it's okay to ask for help. Organizations like Badge of Life[3] may be able to help you identify an officer who is willing to share his or her story.

- **Chaplain support program.** For many officers, religious and spiritual support can boost resilience. The International Conference of Police Chaplains and the American Police Chaplains Association have resources to help you learn more.[4]

- **Annual in-service training to all officers on mental wellness.** Officers may need a regular reminder about what to expect during a critical incident and healthy ways to cope with stress. Supervisors in particular must also understand what their organizational responsibility is and what resources are available when dealing with a peer or subordinate who needs assistance. This education could be integrated with other required training on firearms and use of force.

- **Annual officer wellness checks.** Offering or even requiring an annual appointment with a mental health clinician can give officers who are struggling an opportunity to get assistance and provide others with a refresher on managing stress.

- **Wellness resources and information.** These can help officers learn how to build their own resilience and understand warning signs of a serious problem and how to connect with mental health support. Some officers will learn best by reading, and that information can be shared through agency bulletin boards, newsletters, websites, etc. Some handouts are available at the end of this guide.

---

[3] "Badge of Life," http://www.badgeoflife.com/.

[4] "International Conference of Police Chaplains," http://www.icpc4cops.org/; "American Police Chaplains Association," http://www.americanpolicechaplain.org/.

- **Crisis intervention team (CIT) programs.**[5] These programs provide training for officers on how to respond to a person experiencing a mental health crisis. More important for officer wellness, they provide an opportunity for officers to learn about mental health conditions without being in the spotlight. CIT programs also help create good working relationships with local mental health providers, which are vital in a mass casualty event.

Support the creation of an officer peer support program

Many officers are more comfortable talking to fellow officers than with mental health professionals about stressful or traumatic situations. They feel that only another law enforcement officer can really understand their experiences and stresses. Officers are also often wary of using any mental health services that might appear on their employment or medical record. Well-trained peer support officers can offer confidential support and education, providing officers easy access to help they can trust. Some peer support programs also offer help lines to provide support for day-to-day stresses and teams that can be deployed to the scene of a critical incident.

Peers, if they are trained to notice signs of stress, can also be helpful in proactively reaching out to fellow officers who are struggling. Even when they aren't providing formal support, peers can help create a more supportive, cohesive agency where offers feel comfortable looking out for one another.

But peers need to work hand-in-hand with licensed mental health clinicians to ensure that any officer needing more intensive support can be connected easily. Peers may be able to convince an officer to seek professional support if needed, or provide a testimonial about a particular mental health professional who really understands the concerns of law enforcement.

"I think everybody knows that there are bad things that happen to people, but they need to know there are people out there to help. We need to know early on in our career that we are not alone—other people have been here first, and they can help me through this trauma I have experienced."

— Lieutenant Kit Cummings, Law Enforcement Peer Specialist, Virginia Law Enforcement Assistance Program

---

[5] "Law Enforcement and Mental Health," National Alliance on mental Illness, accessed April 6, 2016, http://www.nami.org/cit.

Much of the appeal of a peer program is that it is driven by officers' needs and concerns, so you cannot force the implementation of a successful peer support program. However, as chief, your endorsement and support is a sign that you care about officers' well-being.

The International Association of Chiefs of Police provides detailed guidelines for peer support programs.[6]

Case study: Police Organization Providing Peer Assistance (POPPA)

After the September 11, 2001 attack on the World Trade Center, police officers in New York City reached out for support from their fellow officers. The Police Organization Providing Peer Assistance (POPPA) organization, an officer peer support program established in 1996, offered a way for officers to connect with someone who understood the stresses of policing without alerting their supervisors or immediate colleagues.

Training for volunteers

POPPA volunteers are active police officers, not mental health professionals. Current volunteers and mental health professionals screen those who wish to join the peer support team. Each new member must undergo eight days of training that includes a focus on communication skills, some practice listening with empathy and without judgment, and information about mental health resources. Peer support volunteers are also trained on how to help a fellow officer access professional mental health services when appropriate and how to handle a crisis situation if one arises. Peers attend training two to four times per year to remain updated on peer support strategies, referral options, and current treatment

Types of supports

POPPA has a 24/7 help line and is staffed to provide a response to callers within 15 minutes. In addition to telephone contact, POPPA provides individual face-to-face peer support and assistance with referrals to mental health professionals and peer-led support groups. When appropriate, volunteers work with mental health professionals to refer to them cases that require further evaluation and treatment.

---

[6] "Peer Support Guidelines," International Association of Chiefs of Police, accessed April 6, 2016, http://www.theiacp.org/ViewResult?SearchID=148.

In addition, POPPA has developed Trauma Response Teams, which respond to certain traumatic events such as shootings, serious motor vehicle accidents, and officer line of duty deaths to provide peer support and psychoeducation regarding traumatic stress, self-care, and when to seek professional assistance. POPPA has also developed an Outreach and Resiliency Support Program, in which peers and a mental health professional provide an overview of job-related and personal stress to a large group of officers. Then a small group meeting provides officers an opportunity to talk about work-related and personal stressors, strategies to cope with stress, and when and how to seek assistance.

Confidentiality

The size of the New York Police Department (NYPD) and the POPPA volunteer network allows the program to provide anonymous support from peer support officers who do not have a prior relationship with the officer seeking assistance. It is important to note that both the client and peer are protected, and any information obtained from their interaction will never become part of a departmental enquiry or investigation or enter an officer's personnel file. This aspect of POPPA may be hard to replicate in smaller departments, and some peer support programs may use external volunteers (such as retired officers) to reassure officers that information that they share will be kept confidential.

Conclusion

The POPPA help line served more than 1,000 officers per year for a few years after 9/11 and continues to serve about 450 officers per year. Another 3,000–5,000 officers are assisted by other POPPA programs each year. It is estimated that POPPA services have prevented at least 80 suicides. Since POPPA's inception in 1996, the suicide rate in the NYPD has dropped approximately 40 percent—from about 22/100,000 to 12–14/100,000 per year. After Hurricane Katrina in New Orleans in 2005, the Boston Marathon bombing in 2013, and the riots in Baltimore in 2015, POPPA provided peer support to police departments in the affected cities and laid the groundwork for local peer support programs. For more information, visit http://poppanewyork.org/.

Reviewed by John Petrullo and Frank Dowling, MD

Find the right mental health service providers to support your officers

If your agency experiences a mass casualty event, your mental health incident commander (described in chapter 3) will coordinate the overall mental health response, but you will need a deeper bench to support all your officers. You also need to ensure the providers you choose have credibility with your officers.

Many officers are uncomfortable asking for help from a mental health professional on the agency's or city's payroll. They worry that the information they share will not remain confidential and could jeopardize their job. On the other hand, officers can also have a hard time connecting with a mental health provider who is not familiar with law enforcement culture. During a critical incident, officers will be more likely to ask for assistance from a mental health provider if they already know and trust the provider. Finding mental health providers who can work successfully with officers can be a challenge, so it's important to reach out to providers in the community now and identify the right individual(s). Look for mental health professionals who

- are familiar with law enforcement culture or are willing to learn;

- have at a minimum a master's degree in a mental health discipline, i.e., social work, psychology, or counseling;

- are properly licensed;

- are trained in trauma care and understand the principles of psychological first aid;

- understand privacy concerns and can guarantee that private information will not be shared;

- are able to interact regularly with officers through training, ride-alongs, investigations, and other activities.

"I bounced back and forth between therapists. It wasn't clicking because the therapist didn't have any police background. I didn't go to the employee assistance provider because they are countywide, not specialized to police. I just wasn't in my comfort zone. . . . I stopped going to therapy and I started looking online. . . . [Later,] I started to go to a support group in central Florida, just cops talking to cops. I found a therapist who is a retired cop."

— *Sergeant Mark DiBona, Deputy Sheriff, Seminole County, Florida*

There are several options to pursue to find the right mental health providers. If your employee assistance provider (EAP) provides licensed mental health professionals, it can be a good choice. However, officers' privacy concerns will have to be addressed proactively, and they will need a guarantee that no information goes back to the agency. Other places to look include the following:

- Police psychologists and other mental health professionals involved in officer training or investigations

- Mental health providers who work with other law enforcement and first responder agencies near you

- Mental health agencies and mental health organizations within your community

- Mental health workers who are former law enforcement or who have a family member in law enforcement

- University and hospital departments of psychology, psychiatry, counseling, and social work

Once you have identified your mental health provider(s), make sure to work with them frequently. The more visible and active these professionals are within the agency, the more comfortable officers will be with them. Involve them in your mental health work group and ask them to assist in reviewing policy and providing education and training.

Review your psychological services policies and procedures

If your agency does not have a policy on psychological support after critical incidents, we recommend you develop one. It can be as simple as stating that any officer involved in a critical incident should meet with the mental health manager (if there is one), a known and trusted mental health professional, or a member of the command staff for informal support. Refer to "How to Assist a Fellow Officer after a Critical Incident" on page 129 for help determining what to say to an officer after a critical incident. Your policy should also describe support resources available to officers on an ongoing basis.

> "We can't continue to treat officers involved in a use of force incident like criminal suspects. Yes, there are parts of investigation that have to occur, but we need to encourage our peers to take time to process, to talk to their families, and to use the support systems they have."
>
> — *Lieutenant Alexander L. Eastman, MD, MPH, FACS, Deputy Medical Director, Dallas Police Department*

Clear communication about new policy

One challenge for chiefs in changing policy is how to communicate about changes to officers. We recommend proactively educating officers about the kinds of flexibility and support you can offer, especially if you are making a change to your current policy. Officers who are used to a particular program of formal support might feel confused or let down if that support changes, even if the changes involve an increase in support options. Make it clear that any changes are designed to improve the support offered and to take advantage of the most effective psychological support available.

Encourage family and peer support, not isolation

We know that support—from friends and family, fellow officers, supervisors, and mental health professionals—and access to personal coping mechanisms is important to resilience and recovery. Most people benefit from time to spend with family, get adequate sleep, and take care of themselves. Ensure that your policies allow officers enough flexibility to take care of themselves and that they do not unnecessarily isolate officers from their peers and families.

Review the research on early formal intervention after traumatic events

You may also want to check in on your current practices regarding debriefings and other forms of formalized early psychological interventions. Currently, there is no formal psychological intervention that has been shown to be effective in preventing post-traumatic stress disorder (PTSD) or other mental injuries in the immediate aftermath of a traumatic event.

Many chiefs are familiar with critical incident stress management (CISM) debriefings, which are a common way to support first responders in the immediate aftermath of a traumatic event. Mental health clinicians and peer support officers using this approach have driven the conversation about officer mental wellness and brought attention to the needs of officers after critical incidents. You may wonder why we aren't wholeheartedly recommending this debriefing technique. It's because debriefings, especially delivered in a single session with no follow-up, are not a panacea. We want to describe the components of interventions based on best practices, rather than focus on a term— *debriefing*—that has come to mean different things to different people.

Various forms of debriefing, with individuals or groups, have been used by law enforcement agencies since the 1980s. There has been confusion about the effectiveness of debriefings. Many people find them a positive experience, but officers who have experienced them do not fare better in the long run than those who have not. And most concerning, a small number of individuals actually do worse after a debriefing. People have different responses to debriefings, and it's not clear why.

Developed in the 1980s by former firefighter Jeffrey Mitchell and George Everly of the Johns Hopkins School of Medicine, the original CISM debriefings followed a set structure that encouraged everyone to share their experiences and emotions while the impact of the trauma was still fresh. They also included a review of the traumatic experience and education about a range of possible reactions to psychological trauma. They were often mandatory. Studies, and then reviews summarizing the findings of more than a dozen studies, have shown that this specific approach and variations of it following similar rules were ineffective and in some cases were even harmful.[7]

One possible explanation of these findings is that when a debriefing is too rigid and scripted, it can compound the trauma some individuals experience. This may be true particularly if the debriefing is mandated for individuals who would rather not attend and requires individuals to retell (and listen to) the details of the incident. Another possible explanation is that learning about all the potential warning signs of a serious mental health problem immediately after a trauma can be self-fulfilling, increasing the chances an officer will develop PTSD down the line.

Based on the evidence showing that people react differently to debriefings, many mental health providers have adapted their approach. In 2007, George Everly co-authored a paper with Jonathan Bisson of Cardiff University, a lead author of the research that raised concerns about debriefings. Both authors suggested an alternative to mandatory debriefings. They suggested that, shortly after the traumatic event, those affected should be provided with empathetic and practical psychological support and with information about possible reactions, about what they can do to help themselves, and about how they can access support from family and community.[8]

At the time, most of the available evidence was from research assessing the impact of individual debriefings—as opposed to group debriefings, which had not been studied as thoroughly. In the years since, further research has reinforced these earlier findings.[9] Research also shows neither early formal psychological nor pharmacological interventions (i.e., medication) have been shown to prevent PTSD or other mental injuries following traumatic events.[10]

---

[7] Suzanne C. Rose et al., "Psychological Debriefing for Preventing Post Traumatic Stress Disorder (PTSD)," *Cochrane Database of Systematic Reviews* 2002, no. 2 (2010), http://onlinelibrary.wiley.com/doi/10.1002/14651858.CD000560/epdf.

[8] Jonathan I. Bisson et al., "Early Psychosocial Intervention Following Traumatic Events," *American Journal of Psychiatry* 164, no. 7 (2007), 1016–1018, http://www.wpic.pitt.edu/Education/CPSP/2%20%20%20IE1%20-%20Bisson%20et%20al.pdf.

[9] Edna B. Foa et al. eds., *Effective Treatment for PTSD: Practice Guidelines from the International Society for Traumatic Stress Studies* (New York: Guilford, 2009).

[10] Jonathan I. Bisson, "Editorials: Early Responding to Traumatic Events," *British Journal of Psychiatry* 204, no. 5 (May 2014), 329–330, http://bjp.rcpsych.org/content/204/5/329.

Implications for tactical debriefings

Note that this research applies only to *psychological* debriefings that include a discussion of officers' experiences—not to *tactical* debriefings that are focused on ensuring communication about facts and other information that is necessary for police work. Tactical debriefings can also trigger a traumatic response and should be delayed if possible.

During a tactical debriefing, it is important to remember that while some officers may freely express their feelings, many people who have been exposed to psychological trauma remain businesslike or even emotionally withdrawn in the immediate aftermath. Therefore, it may be especially difficult to gauge the impact of the discussion on some individuals. Comments and observations, even those that are intended to be reassuring, may spur unexpected reactions that develop into sources of long-term resentments, fears, despair, or anguish.

Whatever model of early support you use, be sure that psychological support is available during and after tactical debriefings to help identify and address negative reactions.

Summary and recommendations based on these research findings

Because the research doesn't explain *why* debriefings have different levels of benefit for different individuals or predict which individuals will react to debriefings in which ways, it's especially important to rely on a trusted and experienced mental health professional to help you navigate this challenge. Together, you can decide what approach is best for your agency. Specifically, we suggest asking your mental health professional to review the research carefully and make recommendations about any needed changes to your current policy and procedure.

In the absence of formal interventions that are proven to work for all people, experts have developed a more flexible, individualized approach built on findings from related research on resilience. Several organizations recommend that early interventions follow these five principles:

1. Promoting a sense of safety
2. Calming
3. A sense of self and community efficacy
4. Connectedness
5. Hope

Psychological First Aid is the most commonly used early intervention based on these principles and has been promoted by the National Institute of Mental Health,[11] the National Center for Post-Traumatic Stress Disorder,[12] and the Cochrane Review.[13] "How to Assist a Fellow Officer after a Critical Incident" on page 129 is based on the concepts of Psychological First Aid.

The good news is that while PTSD and other conditions may not be preventable immediately after a traumatic incident, there are effective treatments that can help individuals who are in distress.

Some options for assisting officers shortly after traumatic incidents

After critical incidents, there is no one-size-fits-all approach that works for every officer. Officers who need support should be able to access it through a variety of means—not necessarily required to participate in a specific intervention. In addition, wellness supports should be ongoing so that officers have access to support at any point, whether immediately after a critical incident or months later.

Here are some options for providing psychological support shortly after a traumatic incident.

On day one, provide brief, flexible one-on-one check-ins

Brief, one-on-one check-ins with officers, ideally before they go off shift on the day of a critical incident, can help officers collect themselves. One model for individual check-ins is Psychological First Aid, which focuses on providing practical support (safety, food, transportation) and offers empathy and suggestions for coping. Psychological First Aid can be delivered by a mental health provider or by anyone else who is ready to listen. The person providing Psychological First Aid offers to listen but allows the officer to decide how much to say about the specifics of the incident. He or she also makes sure that the officer has a number to call day or night to talk with someone who can provide ongoing psychological support.

For more information on how to have these conversations, see page 129, "How to Assist a Fellow Officer after a Critical Incident."

Group educational briefings

Some group meetings can be helpful as long as officers are not asked to retell the story of the event. After mass casualty events with many responders, some agencies have chosen to do educational briefings during which officers learn about mental health supports that will be available to them and

---

[11] "Post-Traumatic Stress Disorder," National Institute of Mental Health, accessed November 30, 2015, https://www.nimh.nih.gov/health/topics/post-traumatic-stress-disorder-ptsd/index.shtml#part_145372.
[12] "PTSD: National Center for PTSD," U.S. Department of Veterans Affairs, accessed November 30, 2015, http://www.ptsd.va.gov/professional/treatment/early/index.asp.
[13] Rose et al., "Psychological Debriefing" (see note 3).

where to call for help. Officers can also be reminded about healthy ways to cope with stress. Finally, officers can be given an opportunity to ask about their reactions—this can help them feel reassured about unexpected reactions they are experiencing.

We suggest *not* listing the "normal" reactions to trauma, because there is such a wide range of reactions. If an officer does not hear his experience on the list, he may worry that something is wrong with him. If you do list possible reactions to trauma, make it clear that almost any reaction is normal at this point (though officers may need help coping with them).

One-on-one wellness checks at least a few days after the incident

Several agencies have offered one-on-one wellness checks with a mental health professional a few days or weeks after a mass casualty event. These conversations can provide information about what services are available, explain how support and treatment are different from fitness-for-duty evaluations, and, most important, stress that mental health treatment is entirely confidential (you as chief cannot know what is being discussed). The checks can be brief, and the mental health professional should take a flexible approach, never forcing the officer to discuss something that they aren't ready for.

Some chiefs have made these check-ins mandatory, with the hope of providing "cover" to officers who really need help—a mandatory check means no officer draws attention by seeking assistance. While mandatory mental health services are generally not recommended,[14] this approach may be helpful if approached carefully. For example, wellness checks should be scheduled *after* the immediate crisis is over. Officers will not be able to focus on their mental health until safety and security are assured, and they may react defensively if the check is too soon.

It can be helpful to describe these checks as an opportunity for officers to ask about any health or wellness issues. For example, some officers may feel more comfortable asking about their children's reaction to the incident or about how to lose weight than discussing their own psychological reactions— and that's okay. Those conversations are an opportunity to build trust so that officers feel comfortable coming back for help if they need it.

Other supports

In addition to the brief interventions already mentioned, officers should also have access to individual support from mental health professionals, employee assistance providers, peer support providers, chaplains, and other programs. With an array of options, each officer is more likely to find what works for his or her individual needs.

---

[14] National Institutes of Mental Health, *Mental Health and Mass Violence: Evidence-Based Early Pyschological Intervention for Victims/Survivors of Mass Violence* (Washington, DC: Government Printing Office, 2002), http://www.nimh.nih.gov/health/publications/massviolence_34410.pdf.

3. Planning the Incident Response for a Mass Casualty Event

Once you are working on a foundation of greater resilience within your agency, there are some specific steps to take to plan for a mass casualty event. Again, even if you do not experience a mass casualty event in your jurisdiction, these steps will help you coordinate with other jurisdictions during any crisis. And if a mass casualty event occurs in a neighboring community, this planning will help you support your neighbors.

Assign a mental health incident commander

To implement your mental health work group's recommendations and really get into shape to deal with a mass casualty event, you will need a highly respected point person on mental health issues. Communities like Aurora, Colorado, and Newtown, Connecticut, found that a trusted mental health professional who knows the agency and law enforcement culture can help build your agency's resilience. He or she can build relationships and credibility now with your officers so that they are comfortable turning to him or her during a mass casualty event.

Identify this individual today, and task him or her with the following:

- Managing all mental health-related tasks during a mass casualty event

- Coordinating with the officer wellness workgroup

- Developing relationships between the agency and mental health service providers

- Reviewing policies and procedures on providing psychological services to officers after a critical incident

- Providing training and consultation for supervisors

- Providing education and support for officers' family members

During a mass casualty event, your mental health manager will serve as an incident commander working with you, your command staff, and mental health service providers to triage for immediate needs and make plans for longer-term mental health supports. He or she will also advise you on operational decisions that may have an impact on officer mental health to avoid unnecessary exposure to trauma and ensure that mental health services support operations rather than hamper them.

"Dr. John Nicoletti and I already had that relationship of trust. So when the theater shooting occurred, I made sure John was called, and he and his team were on site within two hours. They stayed with our cops and civilian members for weeks as we coped with the media crush, the memorials, the funerals and the ongoing devastation we were enduring with the victim families and the community. His team did all kinds of ad hoc, spur-of-the-moment counseling, as well as formal debriefings for our first responders and our victim advocates. They were just "there" all the time, and by always being present, they very much helped us endure and begin to heal.

"Everyone who responded to the theater that night participated in a collective debriefing eight days later. I know there is debate within the professional community as to the value of such debriefings, but in our case this session was powerful and effective, almost certainly because we had Dr. Nicoletti, a true pro and a veteran of the Columbine tragedy, running the debriefing."

— *Daniel Oates, Chief of Police, Miami Beach, Florida,*
and former Chief of Police, Aurora, Colorado

Choose someone thoroughly qualified and suited to the role to serve as your mental health manager. To be most effective both today and in the event of a mass casualty incident in the future, your mental health manager should be

- familiar with the impact of trauma;

- familiar with the principles of Psychological First Aid;

- willing to learn about your agency and get to know commanders, line staff, and union leadership along with operational and support staff;

- integrated into the incident command structure;

- familiar with state, regional, county, and local mental health services.

For many agencies, a licensed mental health provider affiliated with your employee assistance provider (EAP) or a police psychologist may be ideal for this role. Other agencies may use a community mental health provider who is willing to familiarize him- or herself with law enforcement culture or a command level officer with a background in mental health. You may not have the perfect individual, but now is the time to assign these responsibilities and provide training and support.

For more on the mental health incident commander's role during a during a mass casualty event, see the handout on page 125.

Build close partnerships with first responder agencies and other leaders in your community

During and after a mass casualty event, your strongest allies can be the other first responders and community leaders in your community and neighboring communities. It's important to strengthen those relationships now and plan together for responding to emergencies. You should also create a mechanism for resolving different approaches during the incident, to avoid agencies working at odds with one another during a crisis. Unfortunately, lack of coordination during a crisis can have a real impact at the scene and lead to long-term conflict between agencies. For example, the 9/11 Commission Report suggests that additional lives may have been lost during the September 11, 2001 attacks because police officers who passed firefighters in the stairwell of the World Trade Center did not inform the firefighters of instructions to evacuate and because other firefighters were not willing to take evacuation orders from police officers.[15]

Which agencies you need to coordinate with depends on your community's size and location, but here are some stakeholders that are generally involved in an emergency response:

- Neighboring police and sheriff's departments

- Fire and emergency medical services

- Local and state offices of emergency management and victims services

- Municipal, county and state government

- Local emergency response organizations, such at the Red Cross and Volunteer Organizations Active in Disasters

- Faith groups

- Your local, regional, and state departments of health and mental health

- Hospitals and other healthcare providers

- School districts, colleges, and major employers

It is particularly important that you have agreements in place with other first responders about incident command. You may not need formal agreements with schools or employers, but having pre-existing relationships with these groups will make it easier to coordinate during a crisis.

---

[15] National Commission on Terrorist Attacks on the United States, *9/11 Commission Report* (Washington, DC: Government Printing Office, 2004), 553, http://govinfo.library.unt.edu/911/report/index.htm.

"Angel chiefs" after Sandy Hook

by Douglas Fuchs, Chief of Police, Redding, CT

Many years ago, the chiefs of police departments around Danbury, Connecticut, made a pact that if something tragic happened in any of our neighboring communities, we would all respond and do whatever was needed to assist one another and act in a supporting role to see the incident through. You might have a huge department with all kinds of support staff underneath you, but having a peer to be there for you is invaluable for a chief. As a fellow chief, once you show up, the chief knows he is not walking alone.

Six chiefs from neighboring towns responded after the Sandy Hook Elementary School shooting to support the Newtown Police Department. Within 24 hours, we had a schedule in place so that Chief Michael Kehoe was never left alone. He went from place to place with another chief by his side. Other elected officials and department heads started to ask, "Where's *my* shadow?"

After an incident like this, the chief is constantly in meetings, reacting and making decisions 24/7. Chief Kehoe could delegate responsibilities to us. He'd just look at us, and one of us would say, "I got this." Whether it was assisting the Sandy Hook business owners who were financially impacted by road closures and traffic volume, negotiating with national media to relocate television satellite trucks, or (much later on) helping to train others on lessons learned—we were his representatives. Everyone knew if another chief was involved, it was as if Chief Kehoe was there. On the other hand, if we goofed, it was on us.

We also helped listen and process everything that was going on. We all have our own insights, and we all are able to call on additional resources as needed. We provided additional sets of ears, taking some of the pressure off Chief Kehoe. Our only agenda was to focus on him and what he needed to support the community and his officers.

We completely took over the function of coordinating the mutual aid response for Newtown. An independent administration was set up to handle all logistics. Day to day, we would assess the need for additional patrol officers. In addition to regular patrol functions and the need to provide security at all the schools, we looked at what events were taking place and what details needed to be filled. We knew exactly how many officers were required on each shift, and with the assistance of a multitude of other agencies we filled those slots. There was nothing random about officers self-deploying; we had it all scheduled out for 7–10 days in the immediate aftermath of the shooting.

It is so important for agencies, for chiefs, to pre-think this. With the plethora of incidents that are happening each week, it's going to happen in your backyard someday. I cannot overstate how overwhelming a position a chief is in after one of these incidents. Make a pact with your neighboring chiefs *now* that if a horrific event or mass casualty event happens in their community, you will show up—no call necessary. Your presence will be required.

Make a regional or statewide plan

Unless your agency is very large, a mass casualty event will require coordination with other first responder and law enforcement agencies across your region or your state. Keep in mind that any incident of this magnitude that occurs in a neighboring jurisdiction is likely to have an impact on your agency—so it's important to plan the assistance you can *offer* as well as what you can expect to receive.

Specifically, as you plan to address officer mental health, consider reaching out to other agencies in your region and state to discuss the following questions:

- **What mental health resources are available, including peer support teams, police psychologists, and employee assistance providers?** Can an agreement be made now about how to deploy these resources in the event of a mass casualty event? For example, after the Virginia Tech shooting in 2007, the South Carolina Law Enforcement Assistance Program and North Carolina Highway Patrol's Members Assistance Team were able to deploy a team of 25 peer support providers to support officers responding to the event in a matter of hours with a single phone call. This assistance proved vital because local peer support providers were involved in responding to the incident and were not available to assist officers within their own agencies.

- **What kind of mutual aid can your agency expect to provide or receive, and how will that be deployed in a crisis?** For example, the Connecticut Police Chiefs Association is developing a plan to provide a detailed breakdown by severity of the event of how many officers neighboring agencies will provide and the procedure they should follow. The hope is that during an event, the deployment of mutual aid will be swift and seamless. For the sake of officer mental health, having adequate resources and a clear plan is key.

- **How can chiefs in your region support one another in the event of a mass casualty event?** After the Sandy Hook Elementary School shooting, several neighboring chiefs provided round-the-clock support for Newtown's Chief Michael Kehoe and his officers. Among those providing support, Chief Marc Montminy of Manchester, Connecticut, had managed a mass casualty event previously and was able to advise on the lessons he learned about protecting officer mental health. To learn more, see the sidebar "'Angel chiefs' after Sandy Hook" on page 63.

4. Building Your Media Team and Strategy for a Mass Casualty Event

Why you need a media strategy

One of the greatest stressors for chiefs who responded to mass casualty events was their role as gatekeepers of media access. While all chiefs are experienced in providing media briefings, a mass casualty event can draw an unprecedented level of national and international media attention and test the most media-savvy chief.

Media reports inform the community about what happened and create transparency about an incident and its impact. Most reporters will be working to help the wider community understand and process the incident, but there may be exceptions. Regardless, the workload and the unprecedented scrutiny can be very stressful.

A great deal of time and energy is often required to manage the media and respond to inquiries. This may stress your officers and community in several ways, including the following:

- The volume of media requests and the presence of media representatives can create an overwhelming volume of work.

- Officers, victims, and family members may be harassed by members of the media looking for interviews.

- Reporters may disrupt the crime scene.

- Officers may be distressed when their actions or the agency's actions are criticized or reported out of context.

- Officers may be frequently confronted with images and descriptions of the victims and crime scene, or they may be distressed when their loved ones see these images and ask questions.

- Officers may become upset and angry when news coverage of the police response is inaccurate or misleading.

It is important to learn how to work effectively with the media and mitigate any challenges associated with the media's involvement.

News today is disseminated faster, more globally, and on more diverse platforms than ever before. The pitfalls of this new media reality come into sharp view when a major incident occurs. Here are five important insights about modern media and tragedies.

There will be massive media interest

Recent mass casualty events have often been accompanied by immediate and massive media frenzies.. Not just local and national media will swarm your city; you might also see Chinese TV and British newspapers and German bloggers—in short, you should expect media teams from all over the world to show up.

You are in charge of setting the boundaries regarding media engagement, access, and restriction. Develop a detailed media strategy now to prepare for an incident that will attract massive public interest. It will allow you to act swiftly and get a handle on the media chaos early on. For details on building a plan, see "How to plan an effective media strategy" on page 47 and "What to include in your media plan" on page 48.

There will be errors and inaccuracies in media coverage

The first details that emerge in the public after an incident are usually not the most reliable ones. Rumors spread fast. These dynamics have always accompanied tragedies—but now they play out in new ways, with social media often replacing word of mouth, for example.

Don't let initial inaccuracies distract you or your agency; they are an unwelcome but inevitable part of the chaos following a mass casualty event. You can correct errors with consistent messaging:

- Correct errors in every briefing and make sure reporters get the latest facts quickly.

- Remind journalists of their important role as fact checkers and curators of information on social media and the Internet.

- Remind everyone that speculations and premature conclusions backfire and that innocent people may be hurt in the process.

- If major errors are not corrected in a reasonable amount of time, actively approach major news organizations that continue to broadcast inaccuracies and ask for a correction. Use the support of officials and your local news sources if needed.

- Contact a news organization's ombudsperson or a columnist who covers the media. These can serve as internal watchdogs.

There will be intrusive behavior

The police and the press are immediately pitched against each other in the aftermath of a mass casualty event. It is the role of the media to inform the public and to ask difficult questions. It is the role of the police to prioritize the community's safety, the investigation's integrity, and victims' privacy over immediate transparency.

This often results in heated debates about what is intrusive and distasteful in reporting about an atrocity. There are no simple answers to these questions because people's feelings about them depend on factors such as an individual's proximity to the tragedy or their prior experiences with trauma. As we have learned about trauma in chapter 1, a funeral story might be interesting until it becomes clear the person buried was a good friend, at which point the information or photographs may suddenly seem voyeuristic. Similarly, while some people may need concrete images to make the tragic event seem real, others are overwhelmed by graphic depictions.

As chief, you will be among those closest to the tragedy, and you need to be prepared to work with your community leaders on controlling your message and enforcing the boundaries. What is appropriate and what goes too far should be decided by your community.

As always when dealing with media requests, trust your instincts and err in favor of protecting the people in your community from too much scrutiny. While you want to be as open as you possibly can be about details of the investigation and the response to the incident, you also need to be as protective as you can of victims, survivors, and everyone else in your community.

While most journalists will be respectful of victims and their families, some simply will not. For example, in the past, media representatives have posed as family members to gain access to a holding area. Others have obtained personal photos from protected online accounts without permission.

You can take the following steps to deal with intrusion:

- Restrict access to press briefings—just as a news organization can lose its accreditation to attend a trial, it can lose its right to participate in your press briefings.

- Make it clear early on that harassment of victims and violations of privacy laws will not be tolerated.

- Bring a victim advocate or mental health professional to the briefings to describe how specific behaviors are negatively affecting victims and the community.

- Remind media organizations of their own ethical standards by praising those who do the right thing and asking your mayor and other community leaders to do the same.

There will also be important reporting

Given your role in the response to a horrific event, you will likely experience the onslaught of media attention as extremely problematic. It is important to remember that no attention at all would not be beneficial—a respectful public conversation about the incident is important, and insightful media coverage of a tragedy does not have to be voyeuristic or intrusive.

Mass casualty events are of broad public interest for a reason: They are events that rattle a community, a nation, and sometimes the world to its core. If people are capable of shooting children in an elementary school or moviegoers at the cinema, then are we still safe? And what kind of society are we?

While your agency and your community will work hard to maintain some privacy and quiet to begin the painful process of grieving, those watching from the sidelines often need opportunities to talk, inquire, and try to understand what happened. They are looking for answers that help restore a sense of order and predictability or maybe even bring meaning or at least clarifications to a senseless act.

Half of adults in the United States followed news of the Sandy Hook shootings closely, a study by the Pew Research Center found.[16] While there clearly are exploitations of tragedy by both trained and citizen journalists, the majority of coverage is helping the public make sense of a horrific incident.

Social media will play an important role

Today, an incident is often instantly reported. Details about shots being fired or police rushing to a crime scene are shared immediately with the world on social media. What's more, as these are fairly new tools, the ethics and moral boundaries of such sharing are still developing. People who happen to be at the crime scene are the first to broadcast details with little or no context, unaware of the rumors and problems this can create.

This presents several challenges for law enforcement:

- People eager to catch a glimpse may rush to the scene of a crime while a shooter is still at large, not appreciating the danger.

- Survivors may share information about victims from the scene before police can ask them not to and before officers can reach out to families for proper death notifications.

- Family members may see images of their relatives that are disturbing and that police or experienced journalists would not share.

- Worried family members may approach officers in holding areas asking about rumors and half-truths picked up on social media that cannot be confirmed or proven false at the time.

But social media can also be productive:

- Twitter and other social media sites may provide unique, detailed access to information from an active crime scene as the crime continues to unfold (as was the case in the Boston Marathon bombing).

- It is among the fastest ways to spread information about safety and what not to do (in case a shooter has fled the scene and is at large, for example).[17]

---

[16] Pew Research Center, *Public Divided Over What Newtown Signifies: Parents Shield Young Children* (Washington, DC: Pew Research Center, 2012), http://www.people-press.org/files/legacy-pdf/12-17-2012%20Newtown%20release%20NII%20FINAL.pdf.

- It may be the most efficient tool to quickly inform the traditional media and ask them to share important public messages immediately.

- Bystanders' and survivors' posts and images may become important evidence, as they often provide images and details not otherwise available.

To use social media effectively and to your advantage, you need to have accounts on social media platforms like Facebook and Twitter before a crisis occurs. You also need to work on building a following so that people are paying attention to your message. The Police Executive Research Forum has developed guidance on building your social media strategy and using it effectively.[18]

Five things to know about media and mass casualty events

1. There will be massive media interest, and you need to prepare for it.

2. There will be errors and inaccuracies in media coverage, and you can learn how to address them.

3. There will be intrusive behavior, and there are ways to regain some control.

4. There will also be important reporting.

5. Social media will play an important role; you should learn to harness it now.

How to plan an effective media strategy: Be prepared. Be proactive. Own your narrative.

These tips will help you plan an effective media strategy and use the insights discussed earlier to your advantage as you navigate media interest in a mass casualty event.

Assign a public information officer or director of media relations. Just as you need a mental health professional in charge of officer mental health, you need a police media relations professional in charge of handling the media.

Your entire media team needs to be closely involved in planning your media strategy. Share your thinking now and ask for their ideas and suggestions.

---

[17] Edward F. Davis III et al., *Social Media and Police Leadership: Lessons From Boston*, New Perspectives in Policing Bulletin (Washington, DC: National Institute of Justice, 2014), https://www.ncjrs.gov/pdffiles1/nij/244760.pdf.

[18] Police Executive Research Forum, *Social Media and Tactical Considerations for Law Enforcement* (Washington DC: Office of Community Oriented Policing), http://ric-zai-inc.com/Publications/cops-p261-pub.pdf.

Reach out to your local media. Invite your local news reporters to join you for a planning meeting. This will help raise awareness of what the challenges will be. It will educate you and your team about the realities of media needs in the age of social media and educate the journalists about their role and potential missteps in a tragedy. As part of your community, local media often end up taking a leadership role in asking their national and international colleagues to respect boundaries and keep up ethical standards. Building this relationship and awareness now will be crucial.

Map out the possibilities. Look at a map of your community and decide where large numbers of media teams can be held and where you would need to restrict access. Have a map indicating these options ready and easily accessible in case the need arises. *Tip: Mass shooters often are copycats, so look at where your schools, movie theaters, city hall, and other important buildings are located. Where would you put 150 TV trucks close to each of these buildings?*

Identify media relations professionals in your community. Ideally, each victim or affected family would have their own media relations consultant who would help them navigate the sudden public interest, potential misinformation, and advances by reporters. Thinking creatively, other chiefs have used the help of local businesses who have supplied such media professionals to support victims. Are there major employers in town you could ask for this type of support? Identify and approach them now so you have a plan in place—including a list of phone numbers of people to call and bring in—that you can quickly activate when necessary.

Brief your officers on your media strategy. From enforcing rules around access to victims to speaking with survivors about their choices for media exposure to being asked to give interviews themselves, your officers will constantly be dealing with aspects of the media's overwhelming presence. To handle this well, your staff needs to be educated about what media might do, why, and what appropriate responses are. In addition, it is important to share your agency's media strategy so officers don't have to guess in the moment.

What to include in your media plan

Schedule press conferences early and often. Frequent briefings from you, even if there's nothing new to share, will discourage reporters from inappropriately approaching victims, families, and first responders for further information.

Have a blanket statement ready for all staff, such as: "I do not have details yet on what happened, but I know the agency has well-designed contingency plans that allow us to be as responsive as possible in any kind of situation. If you have more questions, please talk to our public relations team." This will help your staff know what to say when approached by reporters in stressful moments. Make sure your plan includes distributing this statement immediately to all personnel during an incident.

Stick to your message: There was a plan in place that allowed you to adapt quickly. Focus on how your contingency plan led to minimizing the harm. Some things always could have been done better during a crisis, and you can acknowledge that—but then return to your message. Keep key staff members in the public eye for at least a week delivering your message and owning the airwaves. Focus on what is known. Respond to speculative questions by identifying them as such and say that you will stick with what is known.

Set the rules of engagement. For example, every TV station will want its own equipment set up. Instead, make them collaborate. For a public appearance by the governor or an important speech by victims, ask one news organization to supply the cable, the next the camera, and so forth so they all own the footage together and you can avoid hundreds of cameras and microphones in the face of survivors.

Feed the media useful information. Since you cannot stop the media machinery from reporting 24/7, work with others in the community to get out the messages that will help your community heal. Your team can set up briefings with experts who can talk about the needs of victims and the community, for example.

Adapt your message for national and international media. National and international media representatives do not have the same relationships with your community as the local press. Ask them to report this incident as if it happened in their own town. Ask them if they would sneak into a funeral to snatch photos if their child's best friend were being buried.

Challenge the media to acknowledge the consequences of harmful reporting.[19] Keep victim advocates and mental health professionals front and center to provide specifics about how harmful reporting affects survivors and families.

---

[19] On the Media, "The Breaking News Consumers Handbook," New York Public Radio, last modified September 20, 2013, http://www.onthemedia.org/story/breaking-news-consumers-handbook-pdf/.

PART THREE.

Managing a Mass Casualty

Event and Its Aftermath

Incident and Aftermath Management Action Items at a Glance

	Managing challenges for your agency and community	**Managing challenges and stressors for officers**	**Managing leadership challenges**
Immediate incident response *(Detailed checklists begin on p. 64)*	• Set up a central command with other first responder agencies (p. 57). • Anticipate a high level of media interest and use a proactive, rather than reactive, media strategy (p. 57). • Proactively manage well-wishers and self-deployed helpers (p. 57). • Prioritize support for victims and their families, but be aware of the toll that working with these families takes on officers (p. 58).	• Assign a mental health incident commander to oversee officer mental health (p. 59). • Make sure someone checks in with every officer on duty before they go off shift (p. 60). • Be transparent about evolving plans for mental health services (p. 60). • Be aware that most officers are in survival mode, trying to ensure their safety and the safety of others (p. 61). • Be aware that reactions to the event will vary widely and that normal reactions can still be upsetting and unexpected for officers (p. 61).	• Seek out assistance from other chiefs, community leaders, and larger law enforcement agencies in your state or region (p. 62). • Stay visible and explain what you are doing to keep everyone safe (p. 62). • Recognize that this event is unprecedented (p. 63).

	Managing challenges for your agency and community	Managing challenges and stressors for officers	Managing leadership challenges

The first weeks	• Manage well-wishers with mutual aid and careful media messaging (p. 69).
	• Stem the flow of donations, and assign a project manager to manage those that arrive (p. 70).
	• Avoid mistrust and tension by continuing to coordinate and communicate with other first responder agencies (p. 70).
	• Develop a proactive, long-term media plan (p. 71).
	• Expect debate and speculation about the cause of the tragedy (p. 72).
	• In responding to Freedom of Information Act (FOIA) requests, be sensitive to officers' needs (p. 72).
	• Anticipate that funerals will be challenging on many fronts (p. 73).
	  ○ Take time and care to ensure memorials and other events are culturally appropriate.
	  ○ Bring in extra hands to get the logistics right.
	  ○ Anticipate the presence of hate groups and protesters, and work to avoid further violence.
	  ○ Have an agency presence at each memorial service.
	  ○ Do not require officers to attend funerals, but communicate clearly about expectations if they do.
	• Be aware that visiting dignitaries and other VIPs may add to your workload (p. 75).
	• Anticipate bomb threats, death threats, "truthers," and conspiracy theorists (p. 75).
	• Expect increased calls for service from a community on edge (p. 76).
		• Add a mental health professional to your team if you don't have one already (p. 76).
		• Make support available to all staff members (p. 77).
		• Ensure that informal mental health support is available at all times (p. 77).
		• Offer one-on-one check-ins with a mental health professional (p. 77).
		• Avoid collective retelling of the events (p. 78).
		• Expect officers to react differently depending on where they were when the event occurred (p. 78).
		• Support officers through a roller coaster of responses to the event (p. 79).
		• Be aware that officers may experience stress and frustration from dealing with the aftermath (p. 80).
		• Address conflicts within the agency and with other first responder agencies before they fester (p. 80).
		• Realize that officers may displace anger onto their colleagues and leaders (p. 81).
		• Take your time deciding how to recognize officers with formal awards and honors (p. 81).
		• Encourage supervisors to look out for their officers (p. 83).
		• Be flexible and look for ways to alleviate the pressure on officers (p. 83).
		• Reach out to officers' families (p. 83).
		• Keep officers as informed as possible (p. 84).
			• Find allies in your community (p. 84).
			• Recognize that your leadership is vital even when another agency is in charge of the investigation (p. 85).
			• Stay alert to conflict within the agency (p. 85).
			• Put your oxygen mask on first (p. 86).
			• Model help-seeking behavior for officers (p. 86).

	Managing challenges for your agency and community	Managing challenges and stressors for officers	Managing leadership challenges
The first months	<ul><li>Work with survivors and families to respectfully clean up temporary memorials (p. 87).</li><li>Call on volunteers to sort donations (p. 87).</li><li>Be aware that investigations and reports can reopen the wounds (p. 87).</li><li>Work with other community leaders to accommodate expanded policing responsibilities (p. 88).</li></ul>	<ul><li>Be aware of emotional exhaustion (p. 88).</li><li>Be aware that serious mental health problems can emerge now, just as things are getting back to normal (p. 89).</li><li>Keep working closely with your mental health team (p. 89).</li><li>Anticipate trauma triggers, and prepare officers to deal with them (p. 89).</li><li>Create a long-term officer wellness plan (p. 90).</li><li>Ensure officers have access to evidence-based services and supports (p. 90).</li><li>Consider setting up a formal peer support network (p. 91).</li><li>Continue education and outreach to officers' families (p. 91).</li></ul>	<ul><li>Adjust your expectations, and get help if the intensity does not let up (p. 92).</li><li>Help officers move forward by acknowledging the toll the event has taken on you (p. 92).</li></ul>
The long haul	<ul><li>Try to make anniversaries a healing event rather than a painful reminder (p. 95).</li><li>Look for opportunities to help the community heal (p. 96).</li></ul>	<ul><li>Be aware that time doesn't heal for everyone (p. 97).</li><li>Anticipate triggering events, and provide support (p. 98).<ul><li>Help officers cope with the trial (p. 98).</li><li>Anticipate the impact of other mass casualty events (p. 99).</li></ul></li><li>Support officers in finding their own ways to remember and cope (p. 99).</li><li>Create a long-term infrastructure to support officer mental health (p. 100).</li></ul>	<ul><li>Attend to your own mental wellness (p. 100).</li><li>Be wary of defining yourself by your crisis leadership (p. 100).</li><li>Reassess you role in light of how this experience has changed you (p. 101).</li></ul>

5. Immediate Incident Response

Managing challenges for your agency and your community

> ➢ **Set up a central command with other first responder agencies.**

One significant challenge for you and your officers during the incident will be coordination with other law enforcement agencies and first responders. Officers from other agencies may self-deploy when their command staff are not present. Conflicting information or conflicting plans of action may be stressful or even dangerous.

If at all possible, set up a central command with other agencies that are responding and make sure your efforts are coordinated. Speak to first responders, victims, family members, and the media with one voice as much as you can. In the midst of a chaotic situation this level of coordination may seem impossible, but there are significant benefits when you can coordinate effectively.

> ➢ **Anticipate a high level of media interest and use a proactive, rather than reactive, media strategy.**

The media response to this event is likely to be bigger and more intrusive than you have ever experienced before. Create a media briefing area right away and provide frequent updates. For more on how to handle the media, see chapter 4.

> ➢ **Proactively manage well-wishers and self-deployed helpers.**

Some communities experience an overwhelming onslaught of well-wishers. Individuals and agencies such as aid groups, clergy, community mental health providers, and well-intentioned members of the public may self-deploy. In most cases, it is best to work with first responder agencies and emergency management organizations rather than individuals. It will be very difficult to vet and coordinate self-deployed responders if they are not affiliated with an existing organization.

Identify an area where they can gather—away from victims and their families—such as a school gymnasium, library, or community center and assign an officer or a volunteer to take their information and assess whether they can be helpful. It is okay to tell them they have to wait or to tell them to go home.

> **Prioritize support for victims and their families, but be aware of the toll that working with these families takes on officers.**

Supporting the families of victims is a huge challenge for you and your officers. Distraught family members will be desperate for and may demand information that you do not have or endanger themselves trying to access the crime scene. Officers assigned to assist the families may face questions they cannot answer. When families are gathered together, information—sometimes inaccurate—may spread about the police response or the welfare of an individual. Families may get very upset if officers can't answer their questions. For example, an officer may know whether an individual was injured or killed but not be able to share that information with family members because the person hasn't been officially identified. At the same time, media, clergy and well-wishers may want access to families that prefer privacy. Officers are in the middle, trying to ensure that families needing privacy can have it and that families that want access to clergy and well-wishers also get their needs met.

Sorting out the facts and informing the appropriate family members in a timely way can be a big stressor for officers. Recommendations for managing this challenge include the following:

- Clear communication. Officers need to know what information they can share and with whom. They also need to know who should have access to the families. Families should receive frequent updates, and these should be given to all the families as a group if possible.

- Officers who were first on the scene or who worked the crime scene should not be reassigned to support families or to conduct death notifications. This can create potential conflicts, where officers have information about the scene that they can't share, and can intensify feelings of guilt about not being able to save a life.

- While it's not always possible, in an ideal world each family would have a private room to gather in and a victim advocate to assist them.

- Clergy, counselors, and other supporters can be in a separate area, available at the families' request. Do not permit a free-for-all, because families may become more distressed if unwelcome help is pushed on them.

Managing challenges and stressors for officers

> ➢ **Assign a mental health incident commander to oversee officer mental health.**

No one would suggest stopping in the middle of a crisis to have a heart-to-heart, but you still need to make sure officer wellness is addressed. You will need help with this task. If you have assigned a mental health incident commander as described on page 37, rely on that individual to advise you on matters related to officer mental health.

If you don't have an existing mental health incident commander, assign someone to be responsible for officer mental health. This individual may only serve in this role for a few days while you set up something more permanent, but assigning someone as soon as possible will help with important tasks in the early days. This person could be any of the following:

- A trusted police psychologist

- A licensed mental health professional

- A licensed employee assistance provider

- A member of your command staff

- A chief from a neighboring community

The mental health incident commander's responsibilities today include the following:

- Monitoring the officers' behavior and verbalizations on scene to see if anyone needs immediate assistance.

- Ensuring that a mental health provider or supervisor checks in with *all* officers and civilian staff before the end of shift. This is not a formal intervention, but anyone conducting these check-ins should receive a copy of "How to Assist a Fellow Officer after a Critical Incident" on page 129, which provides on Psychological First Aid guidance on what to do and say.

- Being available to consult with the chief and command staff.

- Sharing information about available mental health services with officers and ensuring that officers' questions are answered.

- Connecting with officers' family members if needed.

- Coordinating with employee assistance providers and other mental health service providers.

- Managing self-deployed mental health professionals. Unfortunately, it will be very difficult to screen and credential mental health professionals on the spot, so it's unlikely that self-deployed providers will be able to assist on the first day. Keep them from disrupting victims and families, take their information for the future, and tell them to go home.

> **Make sure someone checks in with every officer on duty before they go off shift.**

Before going home on the first day, every officer should have a quick conversation with a colleague or mental health professional to check in about how they are doing. If mental health professionals or trained peer support officers familiar to your officers are not available, supervisors can talk with their staff one-on-one at the end of shift. These conversations do not need to be lengthy or complicated, but they should cover a few basics: safety and immediate needs, helping the officer to connect with family or friends, and letting them know whom to call if they need to talk. Even if mental health professionals are able to connect with an officer, most officers will appreciate this kind of support from some combination of fellow officers, supervisors, and command staff.

For a handout with step-by-step instructions on how to approach these conversations, see "How to Assist a Fellow Officer after a Critical Incident" on page 129. Your mental health incident commander should ensure that all supervisors have a copy of this handout and know they are responsible for their officers. For more information on the research behind this approach, see "Review the research on early formal intervention after traumatic events" on page 31.

Psychological First Aid represents the future of the modern response to the critical incident. It allows officers to help each other in a safe, structured way. It's something we can all grasp and use effectively.

— *Lieutenant Alexander L. Eastman, MD, MPH, FACS, Deputy Medical Director, Dallas Police Department*

> **Be transparent about evolving plans for mental health services.**

Even if you do not yet have a plan for providing officers with mental health services going forward, share whatever information you can. Officers appreciate transparency, even if all you can say is, "We are still working on setting up counseling with the employee assistance provider. We will let you know as soon as possible how to get assistance." It tells them you are concerned about their well-being and working on it.

> **Be aware that most officers are in survival mode, trying to ensure their safety and the safety of others.**

During the incident, your officers are just trying to do their jobs and ensure basic needs are addressed—including their own safety, the safety of others, and the availability of medical assistance. Some officers may not even be aware of having any emotional reaction to their experience until much later. This is called "survival mode."

Depending on the circumstances, survival mode may extend days or weeks— for example, if some victims remain unaccounted for or are still medically unstable or when perpetrators remain at large. In other words, the danger or constant reminders of it have not yet passed.

You can still ask how an officer is doing and provide support—just realize that physical health and safety rather than mental well-being are the top priority now.

> **Be aware that reactions to the event will vary widely and that normal reactions can be still be upsetting and unexpected for officers.**

At the end of the first day—or whenever survival mode ends—many officers will want to go down to the bar and get a few beers. The camaraderie of a night at the bar with other cops may be a healthy way to cope in the immediate aftermath of a crisis—it is when a few drinks become too many or when drinking becomes a habit that problems start.

Other normal reactions to trauma in the first 24–48 hours include replaying and re-imagining the event over and over. Some officers will have insomnia or nightmares or feel like they are on an emotional roller coaster. Some may worry about what to tell their kids and spouses and then say nothing. Spouses often notice right away that the officer has withdrawn, not wanting to burden their family. Others become short-tempered. All of these natural reactions can be short-lived and do not necessarily mean that the person will have any long-term mental health problems.

Some officers will feel fine, and they may even think something's wrong with them *because* they feel fine. But feeling fine is also a normal reaction right after a traumatic event.

Managing leadership challenges

> ➢ **Seek out assistance from other chiefs, community leaders, and larger law enforcement agencies in your state or region.**

Today and going forward, you will face increased demands on you personally and on your agency. You will play a role in everything from responding to the media to communicating with victims' families to reassuring the community. Your leadership is vital in setting the tone for your officers, but you also need help to manage the increased responsibilities and ensure that officer wellness is addressed.

You will receive offers of assistance from a wide variety of sources. You will not have time to sift through all of these offers and respond immediately. Assuming the immediate danger has passed, pause for a moment and decide what sort of assistance you need and seek it out.

Some chiefs said their best ally was a chief from a neighboring agency who shadowed them to meetings, kept track of the moving pieces, spoke with authority, and provided personal support. For example, another chief can help you manage witnesses who are uninjured but still need to be interviewed, establish an outer perimeter, and respond to routine calls for service with his or her own personnel. After the Sandy Hook Elementary School shooting, several chiefs responded to support Chief Michael Kehoe, including Chief Marc Montminy from Manchester, Connecticut, who had experience with a previous mass casualty event. Do not hesitate to identify a trusted colleague and ask him or her to serve in that role.

Other chiefs suggested reaching out to larger agencies in your region or your state to identify mental health resources. Many large agencies have a police psychologist on staff, a peer support team, or access to mental health professionals through an employee assistance provider. Do not hesitate to ask for their help in identifying mental health professionals to assist your agency.

> ➢ **Stay visible and explain what you are doing to keep everyone safe.**

The victims, their families, and the community will be looking to you for reassurance that they are safe and the situation is under control. Your officers will also be looking to you for the same reassurance. It's important that you address these concerns proactively, and even if there's little news to report—for example, when the perpetrator is still at large—it's important to keep everyone informed.

Officers, especially those who responded to the scene, will appreciate if you take time to speak with them individually or as a group. You may wish to call an all-staff meeting or address each shift at roll call. Acknowledging that it's a difficult time and thanking them for hard work will also go a long way to boosting their confidence and easing their concerns.

> **Recognize that this event is unprecedented.**

Just like your officers, you as the chief may be experiencing a wide range of reactions to the event. All the chiefs who contributed to this guide experienced guilt and grief and felt they made mistakes. Recognize that this is an unprecedented event in your career and for your agency and that no one can prepare for every possible scenario. It is normal to take your responsibilities very seriously, but some things are truly outside of your control, and a mass casualty event is one of them.

Containing strong feelings can be important to getting through the crisis, but when the immediate danger has passed, do not be afraid to show your officers that you, too, are affected by the tragedy. You can model professionalism by showing that you can experience emotion without losing your ability to function and lead.

Some leaders in this situation will beat themselves up, thinking they lost control of their emotions when they shouldn't have, but the truth is that everyone has to process their reaction. As a preventive measure, seek out someone to talk with so that you can process in private and avoid a loss of control at the wrong time. If there's not a mental health professional on hand, a fellow chief, your spouse, or a trusted friend can assist you.

Immediate incident response checklists

Immediate incident response checklist:
Operations

Task	Completed
1. Activate your mental health incident commander immediately (see page 37).	☐
2. If you don't have a mental health incident commander, assign someone to be responsible for officer mental health. *Tip: This person can be a member of your command staff, a licensed behavioral health professional affiliated with your employee assistance provider, a police psychologist, or a chief from a neighboring agency. If needed, ask a neighboring agency to "lend" you their police psychologist or a mental health professional affiliated with their employee assistance program.*	☐
3. Assign the mental health incident commander to meet with self-deployed mental health responders, take their contact information, and then send them home.	☐
4. Set up a central command with other agencies that are responding and make sure your efforts are coordinated as much as possible.	☐
5. Together with other the leaders of other responding agencies, speak to first responders, victims, family members, and the media with one voice.	☐
6. Once the threat is neutralized, give the first responders the option of some time off.	☐

Immediate incident response checklist:
Getting the help you need and managing self-deployed responders

Task	Completed
1. Ask a chief from a neighboring agency to shadow you, take notes, and help sort and delegate tasks.	☐

2. Request mutual aid from other agencies. Neighboring chiefs can take on the following assignments:
 	
    a. Establishing a perimeter
    b. Creating designated areas for media and well-wishers
    c. Assisting and interviewing uninjured witnesses
    d. Administering the mutual aid response for at least the next week
	☐

3. If needed, contact a larger police department in your state that has an employee assistance provider or police psychologist who can offer guidance about how to support your officers. *Tip: A community-based mental health provider may be helpful, but you really want to identify someone familiar with law enforcement culture.*	☐

Immediate incident response checklist:
Support for victims' families

Task	Completed
1. Work with victim assistance specialists in your community as much as possible.	☐
2. Work closely with the coroner or medical examiner to identify victims quickly so that the families can be informed.	☐
3. Assign a private space, if possible, for each family to gather.	☐
4. Create separate holding areas for victims' families, the media, and self-deployed helpers (clergy, mental health providers, and other groups).	☐
5. Tell family members that clergy and counselors are available at their request.	☐
6. Ask victim advocates to educate families about their rights in interacting with the media.	☐
7. Make sure that officers assigned to assist victims' families have clear instructions about what they can and cannot say to distraught family members. *Tip: If possible, officers should receive guidance from someone trained in victim assistance.*	☐
8. Do not assign officers who were part of the initial response or who worked the crime scene to support victims' families or conduct death notifications.	☐

Immediate incident response checklist:
Managing the media

Task	Completed
1. Print out your media plan. If you do not have a media plan, see page 48 for what to include in your plan.	☐
2. Be proactive rather than reactive in managing your response to the media.	☐
3. Update the media regularly even if there is nothing new to report.	
4. Create an area reserved for media away from the crime scene and victims' families.	☐
5. Assign a media liaison and direct all contacts to him or her. Instruct officers to direct all media inquiries to the media liaison.	☐
6. Remind the media to be respectful and maintain boundaries when it comes to victims and their family and friends.	☐
7. Consider whether there's anything the media can do for you. If there's something you need the community to do, such as a particular need that can be fulfilled, get the word out through the media.	☐

Immediate incident response checklist:
Supporting officer wellness

Task	Completed
1. Instruct supervisors to make sure each officer and civilian staff member has a brief personal contact and check-in before they go off shift today.	☐
2. Give every employee the name and phone number of your mental health incident commander or a licensed mental health professional in case they need to talk.	☐
3. Do not require the first-on-scene officers to file their reports on the day of the incident. *Tip: After a traumatic incident, an officer's memory will be clearer after a night of sleep, and filing the report on the day of the event may cause unnecessary stress.*	☐
4. If your plan for providing officers with mental health services is still evolving, tell officers that their well-being is important to you and that you are working on making mental health support available to them. Share whatever information you have at each point.	☐
5. Do not assume that you know who will need assistance. Anyone in your department, from officers to dispatchers to administrative staff, could need mental health support.	☐

6. The First Weeks: From Chaos to a New Normal

Managing challenges for your agency and your community

It may seem that the challenges in the aftermath of a mass casualty event are primarily logistical and operational rather than mental health-related. The fact is that managing the overwhelming demands on your agency effectively is incredibly important to your officers' well-being. They will need time, space, and consistency to recover, and you can help provide that with your leadership. This can be an overwhelming time and there is no perfect or one-size-fits-all approach that works for every agency; following are some challenges other chiefs faced and how they managed them.

> ➤ **Manage well-wishers with mutual aid and careful media messaging.**

Many high profile events gain national and international attention, which means you may have hundreds or thousands of well-wishers in your city offering to help or creating impromptu memorials. Your agency is in charge of handling the logistics of such a massive emotional outpour. Initially this may be reassuring to your community, but self-deployed responders and well-wishers quickly become a huge burden. All the help you receive can lead to such a depletion of time and resources that it has been called a "secondary disaster."

How do you keep all the well-meaning people away from survivors and families, who need privacy? How do you keep well-meaning visitors safe? How do you manage when your visitors block traffic, making it nearly impossible for residents to get around their own community? How do you ask the well-wishers to go home so that the community can have some privacy to begin healing?

Some tips for managing these logistics include the following:

- Continue to accept mutual aid to manage security, traffic control, and other needs.

- Ask for respect for the grieving families and the community.

- Work with other community leaders to strategize about outside visitors. Is there a message you can get out through media—for example, ways that people can help while staying at home?

> **Stem the flow of donations, and assign a project manager to those that arrive.**

People who feel compelled to help will also send donations, monetary and otherwise. In Newtown, Connecticut, the volume of donations was overwhelming. The community received more than 63,000 stuffed animals and between 150,000 and 200,000 pieces of mail, along with pallets of books, school supplies, and backpacks. In Oak Creek, Wisconsin, after the Sikh Temple shooting, the police department began receiving financial donations from Sikh communities in India designated for the officer who was injured during the incident. The department had to open new bank accounts to hold that money on the officer's behalf while he was recovering from his injuries.

Your department will likely be the recipient of many donations, including food, flowers, money, and letters of appreciation. Tips for managing donations include the following:

- Communicate early and often through the media which specific types of assistance are needed and that other efforts, though well meant, are complicating things for your community.

- Ask well-wishers to donate to a cause in their local community or to a well-established relief organization.

- Identify someone to serve as a project manager for sorting donations. Reach out to local businesses and emergency management agencies to find the right person or use a competent volunteer.

"The donations came in tractor-trailer trucks."

— *Michael Kehoe, Chief of Police (ret.), Newtown, Connecticut*

> **Avoid mistrust and tension by continuing to coordinate and communicate with other first responder agencies.**

There is often a "honeymoon" period in the immediate aftermath of large-scale tragedies—the community comes together and first responders of all sorts are lauded as heroes. Everyone works together for the good of the community. Over time, however, it is common for some of these agencies to become distrustful and even hostile towards one another, especially when insufficient communication and coordination lead to conflicting plans or duplication of effort.

Because everyone is under incredible stress, some tension is inevitable. But effective coordination, communication, and teamwork are essential not just to the success of the overall response but also to the resilience of all involved.

➤ Develop a proactive, long-term media plan.

After the first 48 hours, it will be clear how much media attention your incident is attracting. You will have created your media holding area and be controlling your message about your response (for details, see chapter 4.) The question is how long the media will stay. This cannot be predicted: In Newtown, Connecticut, reporters were on site constantly for six to eight weeks after the Sandy Hook Elementary School shooting. After the Manchester, Connecticut, workplace shooting at Hartford Distributors in 2012, the initially strong media response tapered off after a few days. As these events become more frequent, the focus of media attention may shift more quickly to the next event or threat.

A continued strong media presence can be frustrating for residents and officers alike. There is a variety of approaches to interacting with the media. The most important thing is to have a proactive strategy. If you are simply reactive, your agency will become overwhelmed with requests.

Review "What to include in your media plan" on page 48 for strategies to promote a good working relationship with the media and mitigate any negative impact on victims, survivors, yourself, and your officers.

In responding to the media, my highest priority was achieving justice for the victims. I didn't want to misstep and provide reporters with any information that would make it harder to have a successful criminal prosecution. We also adopted the mindset that the media was a tool for us to get the community the information they needed to know about the event, and to be reassured that it was handled well. Provided we stuck to that agenda, we didn't feel compelled to answer their endless questions.

— *Daniel Oates, Chief of Police, Miami Beach, Florida, and former Chief of Police, Aurora, Colorado*

Responding to media requests after the Hartford Distributors shooting

In the aftermath of the Hartford Distributors shooting, Chief Marc Montminy and other community leaders took a novel approach to addressing media requests. Because the perpetrator was deceased and there was no reason to withhold information, they decided to release all the documentation about the shooting to the media with the exception of graphic images of the victims and the crime scene. They called a press conference and gave each reporter a DVD with all the information. This proactive approach effectively ended the rush to uncover information and the story quickly faded from the spotlight.

➢ **Expect debate and speculation about the cause of the tragedy.**

Elected leaders, pundits, or the media will consider this an important time to address the political debate about the causes of the tragedy: Was it lax gun control laws, or should people have easier access to weapons to defend themselves? Was the cause inadequate mental health services? Could better policing or different laws have prevented the incident? Your community may still be burying the dead and resent the spotlight and pressure to engage in these discussions.

If your investigation is ongoing, your inability to share information about the perpetrator will frustrate representatives of the media and may lead to further digging for details. Some things you can do include the following:

- With other community leaders, ask for respect and time to mourn.

- Clearly explain the reasons why some information cannot be shared.

- Stick to you media plan and don't speculate when the facts aren't clear.

- Continue to reassure your community about the things you are doing to keep everyone safe.

➢ **In responding to Freedom of Information Act (FOIA) requests, be sensitive to officers' needs.**

It is typical for law enforcement agencies to receive many FOIA requests after a mass casualty event, starting on day one and picking up in the first weeks. They can come from media representatives and from citizens determined to uncover the "real" story.

When information pertaining to particular officers, such as videos or documents, is released, the officers may be subject to intense scrutiny. This is immensely stressful for the officers. To alleviate this stress and protect officers' privacy, you should do the following:

- If at all possible, give the officers an opportunity to see videos or read documents before they are released.

- Remind officers to secure their social media accounts and the accounts of their family members prior to the release of information to protect their privacy.

- Instruct your mental health team to reach out to the officers to provide support.

> **Anticipate that funerals will be challenging on many fronts.**

Take time and care to ensure memorials and other events are culturally appropriate.

In the rush to accommodate visiting dignitaries and show the community that they are taking action, some community leaders are hasty in planning memorials and other events. It's important to ensure that you are being sensitive and culturally appropriate for the victims and their families. This is particularly true when the incident occurs in a cultural community center, such as a place of worship or a school. You may find yourself caught in the middle trying to mediate these decisions.

The best way to ensure that your agency is sensitive to any issues is to talk with leaders of the affected community and to take sufficient time to understand everyone's needs and preferences.

Respecting the Sikh community's customs in Oak Creek

After the Sikh Temple of Wisconsin shooting, the Sikh community wanted small, private memorials; their custom is not to have expressions of grief in public. Unfortunately, there was pressure for large public funerals with VIPs in attendance. Although the large funerals went forward, the police chief advocated on behalf of the Sikh community and built a lasting relationship based on understanding and support of their customs.

Bring in extra hands to get the logistics right.

Your agency will need to manage logistics around the funerals—clearing roads, providing police escorts, getting people safely in and out of the buildings, keeping media at bay, and providing security for high-profile visitors. In extreme cases when there are multiple funerals in one day, your attention to these logistical concerns can have a real impact on the families. For example, if the memorial services are delayed because there's not sufficient security for a visiting dignitary, it can be very upsetting to families. Again, mutual aid can help fulfill staffing needs for these events.

Anticipate the presence of hate groups and protesters, and work to avoid further violence.

Funerals can also draw the attention of hate groups and other extremists who are looking for a platform to showcase their ideologies. While nothing could be more infuriating than disrespecting grieving families, it is important to make sure that protesters, community members, and officers remain calm to prevent further violence.

Have an agency presence at each memorial service.

As a community leader, you or your command staff should be visible at the funerals. Your presence can be comforting for the families and your community. As these events may be very painful, consider dividing up the ceremonies with your command staff so that no one has to go to every memorial.

Do not require officers to attend funerals, but communicate clearly about expectations if they do.

For officers not involved in managing logistics at a specific funeral, we recommend not making attendance mandatory. Some officers will want to go and may find it comforting. For others, it may be torturous to interact with the family of someone whose life they couldn't save. It's important to inform officers of the schedule of services, that they have a choice whether or not to attend, and whether there is any protocol they should follow if they attend.

The impact of interacting with families of victims cannot be overstated. There were police officers who would have preferred to be involved in the active shooter situation [rather] than going to the funeral. They were more concerned about facing the families of people they could not save than going into a dangerous situation.

— *Marc Montminy, Chief of Police, Manchester, Connecticut*

> **Be aware that visiting dignitaries and other VIPs may add to your workload.**

When a high-profile event occurs, state and national leaders may visit to console families, show their support, and draw attention to a political issue that they believe is the cause of the tragedy. These visits add intensive security requirements and other tasks to your agency's workload. For example, after the Aurora, Colorado, movie theater shooting, President Obama visited with the injured and the families of the dead. Afterward, his office asked local officials to provide a list of the names, addresses, and relationship of key family members of all the victims so that he and the First Lady could write personal letters of condolence. It was a difficult and time-consuming task for the police department, but it was a vitally important service to the victims. A letter from the President of the United States is a powerful statement of the nation and a part of the long-term healing process for the victims and their families.

> **Anticipate bomb threats, death threats, "truthers," and conspiracy theorists.**

Just as the spotlight on your community may draw the attention of hate groups, trouble-makers may also take advantage of the perception of chaos to make your job more challenging. Schools, churches, police stations, and other public buildings may be the targets of bomb threats. Public officials, survivors, and victims' families may receive death threats.

People from outside the community, driven by distrust of the government or extreme ideology, may claim that the incident never occurred or that there was a vast government cover-up of the real incident. They may claim to know the "truth" and broadcast bizarre misinformation. For them this may be idle speculation covered by the anonymity of the Internet. For your community it is salt on the wounds.

The "flavor" of this unwanted attention is different depending on the incident. For example, after the Hartford Distributors shooting, White supremacists protested and sent hate mail because the shooter was Black. You may get threats that someone is going to "finish the job" or accusations that police officers killed the victims and there was a cover-up. Some agencies investigate hundreds of such threats in the weeks, months, and years after the event. For particularly high profile incidents there doesn't seem to be any end—some students injured in the Columbine High School shooting in 1999 continue to receive unwanted communication more than 16 years later.

> Whenever you have sustained media attention on a community, it will draw the attention of a certain element of society that is very suspicious of the government.
>
> — *Michael Kehoe, Chief of Police (ret.), Newtown, Connecticut*

You cannot ignore these threats, or you run the risk of normalizing this behavior. Some harassers have been successfully apprehended. Reach out to federal law enforcement agencies, including the Federal Bureau of Investigation (FBI) and U.S. Marshals Service, for help identifying where threats are coming from, and access to technical experts and behavioral scientists.

> ➢ **Expect increased calls for service from a community on edge.**

After a mass casualty event, everyone in the community is on edge and may be hypervigilant about potential threats. Expect increased calls for service. For example, after a workplace shooting, you may receive calls for assistance when a local company has plans to fire or lay off employees in the worry that such employees may return to take revenge. Following a school shooting, school staff may be more likely to call 911 when they see a stranger or unattended package near the school.

To allay the community's concerns, it's important that your leadership is visible and that you communicate all the things you are doing to keep the community safe.

Managing challenges and stressors for officers

> ➢ **Add a mental health professional to your team if you don't have one already.**

As chief, you likely do not have the training to evaluate mental health services and service providers. You also may not know who could benefit from professional support or how to encourage them to seek it out. And you do not have the time.

If you haven't already, now is the time to bring in a mental health professional who can coordinate services for you and set up an appropriate support structure that makes it most likely that officers will take advantage of the services that are available. This individual will be your mental health incident commander. In the first 24–48 hours, you can assign anyone you trust these responsibilities, but going forward, expertise matters. For more information about what to look for in a mental health incident commander, see "Assign a mental health incident commander" on page 37.

> You need a licensed mental health provider who knows the law enforcement culture and knows trauma, including the principles of Psychological First Aid. Lots of mental health providers think they are good at everything, but if you think that, you're probably not doing anything very well.
>
> — *Jim Rascati, LCSW*

> **Make support available to all staff members.**

Because there is such a variety of reactions to traumatic experiences, anyone in your department, whether they were on-scene during the incident or not, may be affected. Some staff may react more strongly than you expect because of difficulties outside of work or previous experience with traumatic events. This is why frequent casual check-ins with all staff members in the first weeks are essential.

If time and resources are limited, staff members who were closest to the event should receive support first. For example, you may want to check in with staff in this order:

- First responders to the scene

- Officers who were on-scene and arrived after the violence was over, including those assigned to work with victims, their families, or the media

- Detectives assigned to process the scene

- Dispatchers, other civilian staff, and anyone who was off duty

> **Ensure that informal mental health support is available at all times.**

Conversations about traumatic experiences don't have an on and off switch. Ideally, an officer or staff member should be able to reach a supportive listening ear—a trained professional or a peer—whenever they are ready. This means that officers have a phone number to call and also that mental health staff are integrated into your day-to-day operations so officers have many opportunities to become familiar with them. Having mental health professionals at roll-call, during trainings, and during briefings builds the credibility of your mental health team and provides officers with easy access to them.

At the same time, there need to be frequent, casual check-ins with all staff members. In addition to mental health professionals, instruct supervisors to continue to check in with front-line staff, and alert the mental health incident commander if there is a serious concern.

> **Offer one-on-one check-ins with a mental health professional.**

Offer one-on-one coffee or other informal meetings with a trained mental health professional. Make sure it is clear that this is not a physical and not an official fitness-for-duty test—just a conversation with someone trained to help officers cope with their response to the situation. Every officer should have at least one such conversation within the first days or weeks following a mass casualty event. Some chiefs choose to make this mandatory so that officers who are hesitant to ask for help can have some cover with their peers.

> The people who really need support don't take advantage of it. At Aurora, we had a list of every person who responded in the theater. I divided them up among my staff and every officer had to talk to someone at least once. We didn't wait for them to come to us.
>
> — John Nicoletti, PhD

➤ Avoid collective retelling of the events.

If you have mandatory group meetings early on, focus on the psychological impact and educate your officers about how acute stress affects the body, ways to stay resilient, and where to seek support. It may not be possible to stop officers from sharing their experiences, but if they start down that track, suggest they meet separately to continue their discussion. Keep in mind that some officers will be upset to hear details, but they may not feel free to speak up. Make sure officers know that someone is always available if they want to talk about the experience one-on-one.

If possible, consider delaying tactical debriefings. Because of the emotional impact, any officers will not have enough perspective to engage in a "lessons learned" discussion productively. Such a debriefing done too soon may intensify feelings of helplessness and guilt. When a tactical debriefing is scheduled, strongly encourage officers to attend, but do not make it mandatory. A mental health professional or mental health incident commander should be available during any tactical debriefings.

➤ Expect officers to react differently depending on where they were when the event occurred.

Officers may experience a wide variety of reactions related to their assignments on the day of the event. Some officers would rather have worked the crime scene than have been responsible for assisting victims' families, especially while the families were waiting for news of their loved ones' well-being. Officers who were doing crowd control or responding to ordinary calls for service may feel like their contributions were not important. Officers who were off duty or on vacation may feel out of place because they did not share in the experience and did not contribute.

> Imagine the most important event in your career, and you were on vacation. Part of an organization is shared experience. If you were the odd guy who happened to be in Disneyland, then you come back and you can't relate to what happened.
>
> — Marc Montminy, Chief of Police, Manchester, Connecticut

First responders may be worried about the people who were injured. Civilian employees tasked with holding down the fort and fielding hundreds of calls may be overwhelmed or feel their contributions went unrecognized.

When you are assigning responsibilities, account for the officers' roles on the day of the incident. For example, first responders should not be assigned to assist victims' families or required to attend funerals. Officers who were off duty may actually appreciate the opportunity to take on those roles as it helps them contribute meaningfully. Dispatchers and other civilian employees may need more support and flexibility than you expect.

> ### ➤ Support officers through a roller coaster of responses to the event.

For many officers, the emotional roller coaster that started immediately after the event will continue in these weeks. Individual reactions to traumatic events and acute stress vary greatly and can change quickly. The important thing for everyone to remember is that our brains and our bodies are processing the experience, and a whole range of normal responses are expressed: Numbness, grief, guilt, anger, sadness, and many other confusing emotions are all normal reactions. Some officers may feel fine but worry that something's wrong with them because they feel fine.

Some officers may start asking "why" questions. "Why did the perpetrator kill innocent people?" "Why did I live when others did not?" "Why did God allow this to happen?" These questions generally do not have simple answers, and officers may frustrate themselves trying to make sense of an event that has no easy explanations.

Officers' reactions to the event may affect how they work. For example, some officers will want to work around the clock. Others will not leave an injured colleague's hospital bed. Some will take a day off and then find it hard to return. Those who were off duty when the event happened may overwork themselves trying to make up for the guilt they feel about being unable to help during the incident.

Everyone will try to suck it up and do their jobs, but for some that will be difficult. To the degree possible, offer flexibility and encourage all officers to take care of themselves.

An officer walked up to me in the weeks after the shooting and asked, "Chief, when does it stop?" I said, "It doesn't stop. But there are professionals out there that can help you. To help make a plan for you to move forward."

— *John Edwards, Chief of Police, Oak Creek, Wisconsin*

> ### Be aware that officers may experience stress and frustration from dealing with the aftermath.

As if it wasn't enough to cope with the aftereffects of witnessing violence, officers are probably also experiencing stress that has less to do with the event and more to do with the aftermath. Your officers will want to work hard, to contribute, and to support the community, but dealing with the logistical challenges can be incredibly frustrating. Rather than moving the community forward, it can feel like the community has been overrun by an occupying force and their job is just to stem the tide. Officers may resent assignments that feel frivolous, such as escorting a visiting VIP or handling crowd control.

The overwhelming media presence—rehashing of every detail of the event, digging into the back story of the perpetrator, scrutinizing the details of the police response—is often torturous for officers and community members. The same is true for the constant crowd of well-meaning community members bringing food and gifts. Taken together, these constant reminders can actually trigger a trauma response for some officers and members of the community. This influx can make healthy coping mechanisms—such as going for a walk outside and staying away from images of the incident—unavailable. Without a break, there is no opportunity to heal and move forward.

Misreporting and inappropriate behavior by media representatives can also contribute to officers' nagging sense that the world is not as trustworthy as it used to be or that things are not as controllable as they used to be. They can add to the struggle to maintain a sense of hope and control in the aftermath of a great atrocity—all of which can wear down resilience.

> ### Address conflicts within the agency and with other first responder agencies before they fester.

Within your agency there may be conflicts around overtime, time off, and worker's compensation. Officers may be upset if someone takes time off and perceive that as weakness or slacking off. One first responder agency, or staff members within a particular agency, may feel that other first responders are not pulling their weight and are instead taking advantage of the situation to get maximum time off or to set the stage for a disability claim down the line. While there may be an occasional abuse of the system, for officers who truly need time off or psychological support there may be unnecessary pressure to show up as usual or even work extra.

Officers may also bond with those who shared a similar experience that day—with those who responded first feeling more entitled than those who were off duty or responded later. This can cause great conflict within an organization.

Resentment can also arise around awards and honors. Officers in one agency may feel that other first responders are inflating how important their role was in responding to the incident or that particular responders are being singled out for heroic actions when others are not. For guidance on how to award honors sensitively, see "Take your time deciding how to recognize officers with formal awards and honors" on page 81.

Conflicts can also arise around gifts and donations that come to the agency. Well-meaning community members will send tickets to a ball game or trays of food, and officers can get upset if someone seems to take (or be given) more than their fair share. They might ask why, if there were only a limited number, did the gifts go to officers who weren't even on scene that day?

Some tips for managing these conflicts include the following:

- Set a professional example when interacting with other agencies. If there is a persistent conflict, sit down with other agency heads to hash it out, and then tell your staff how the conflict has been resolved.

- Remind officers that anyone could have been a first responder, and that while we should support those that were, there are no "Ground Zero Heroes."

- Even when conflicts seem petty, take officers and their concerns seriously. For example, think carefully about how to distribute gifts fairly and explain your reasoning.

> **Realize that officers may displace anger onto their colleagues and leaders.**

Sometimes when people are upset about something they cannot change—like the fact that someone killed people in their community—they will take out their anger and frustration on things that can change. It's a lot easier to get angry with a living person or with a frustrating situation than with a deceased perpetrator. This is called displaced anger, and it is a very common response when people feel that a situation is chaotic or out of control. Displaced anger can be directed at you as the chief, your command staff, other community leaders, or colleagues and other first responders.

> **Take your time deciding how to recognize officers with formal awards and honors.**

In the aftermath of a mass casualty event, it is entirely appropriate to thank your staff for their hard work and dedication, to take extra time listening to their concerns, and to provide time off if possible. Officers expect and deserve recognition for their contributions and sacrifices. But take your time before giving out awards or honors.

These incidents will garner an unusual amount of political pressure and attention from the media, pushing you to honor officers more quickly and with more pomp than usual. Under that kind of pressure, it can be hard to find the right way to recognize officers and there are good reasons to be cautious.

Challenges and concerns related to officer wellness and awards

In some circumstances, award ceremonies can actually make officers feel worse about their involvement in the incident. Some challenges that have arisen after mass casualty events include the following:

- Some officers are uncomfortable with the attention of an award ceremony and with being called a hero. When others died, officers may feel like their heroism was not adequate or important.

- Some officers may not want to hear about the details of the incident again, even in the context of an award ceremony.

- With so many responders playing important roles, it is hard to draw the line between who should be recognized and who should not. Officers or civilian staff who were involved in the incident response but who were not injured and did not save lives may feel resentful if their role is not recognized.

- If the award ceremony includes other first responder agencies it will be very hard to recognize all the individuals that contributed to the incident response, and there's a good chance of inadvertently leaving someone out.

There's no perfect approach, but there are some lessons learned

There is no perfect formula for crafting an award ceremony that works for everyone. These recommendations and examples can help you think through your options:

- **Don't assume you know what the officers would appreciate.** Ask them for input so they will be more comfortable with the final decision.

- **Do not cave to political pressure to honor officers if you don't think it will be appropriate or respectful.** Well-meaning community leaders may want you to throw a huge award ceremony very soon after the event. Sometimes these events can be comforting for the victims and the community, but that needs to be carefully balanced with the potential negative impact on officers being honored. Instead of making a quick decision, give yourself time to think through your options and consult with the officers involved.

- **Think of the award ceremony as an opportunity for healing.** Even during an award ceremony, you can acknowledge the pain and grief officers may have experienced and make a public statement of support. You may also consider whether there is a beloved local celebrity who could present, making the award ceremony special to the officers. Alternatively, a representative of the affected families who could speak, making the honors more personal.

- **Consult with your mental health incident commander** before any award program. He or she may be able to identify individual officers who will be negatively affected by an award ceremony and help you navigate appropriate awards. Include him or her in the room during the ceremony.

- **Inform officers of any award ceremonies** so they are not surprised.

- **Do not make attendance at award ceremonies mandatory.** Make the agenda clear and tell officers they can opt out of attending.

- **Incorporate awards for the incident in an annual ceremony.** The honors for the incident response can be included in the overall ceremony but should not be the centerpiece. In Newtown, Connecticut, Chief Kehoe made attendance at the annual award ceremony voluntary and gave officers the option to leave prior to the awards for response to the Sandy Hook Elementary School shooting.

- **Give a certificate of appreciation to every officer and civilian staff member involved in the incident response.** By recognizing everyone, you acknowledge the vital roles played by all members of your agency and remind everyone how they pulled together to provide a service to their community. This may also be helpful when there's internal conflict among officers about who is a "hero" and who is not.

- **Give appreciations in private.** If an officer is not comfortable with a public ceremony, you can express the agency's thanks personally and in private.

- **Consider offering a variety of awards** beyond those for lifesaving or for injury in the line of duty. For example, dispatchers may be recognized for calm and professionalism, or officers who conducted death notifications may be recognized for compassion and support to families.

> **Encourage supervisors to look out for their officers.**

Supervisors are in a good position to notice if an officer is struggling. Instruct supervisors to watch for signs that an officer needs help and to discuss their concern with the officer. There is a lot of work to do, but supervisors should have as much flexibility as possible to give officers time off or change assignments if an officer requests it.

> **Be flexible and look for ways to alleviate the pressure on officers.**

When possible, provide officers with some opportunity to control their time—find ways to pay for vacation time or overtime if working more or less is helping some staff cope. You may need to continue to cover shifts with mutual aid from other agencies. Consider also giving the entire agency a day off or extending holiday vacation time.

> **Reach out to officers' families.**

Officers' spouses and children often need education and support when an officer has experienced a trauma. They are also a good source of information. Some agencies have conducted a brief anonymous online survey of family members asking for their observations. This can help identify whether officers or families need additional support.

Also, encourage officers to connect with family and to talk about their experiences. Include spouses and other family members in significant agency events.

> **Keep officers as informed as possible.**

Officers will appreciate regular updates on a variety of topics. In the absence of information rumors may start, or officers may worry unnecessarily. You may want to brief officers on the following topics:

- The status of the investigation, especially if another entity, such as a federal law enforcement agency, is in control of the investigation. Officers may be frustrated or angry if there are developments they learn about on the evening news. Push respectfully for regular updates and pass that information on to officers.

- Information leaked to the media, especially if it includes information about specific officers. For example, if video footage of an officer being injured is released, give the officer an opportunity to warn friends and family to not watch the news if the footage might be disturbing.

- The status of victims who were injured. First responders who assisted the injured may find it helpful to meet with them in person to be reassured that everyone is okay.

Managing leadership challenges

> **Find allies in your community.**

As chief, you should know all the players in your community so you can bring your leadership to the overall community response.

If you haven't already, start lining up allies in addition to your command staff. Your team should include people you trust and can rely on, such as a mental health professional who is serving as your mental health incident commander or a fellow chief from a neighboring community. Another chief may be particularly suited to shadowing you during the day-to-day and helping you prioritize, delegate, and execute in the face of too many competing demands.

Other chiefs have also found it helpful to get support from city government and elected officials. Pay them a visit—from the mayor to the health department to city engineers—during the first weeks following the incident to answer questions and identify ways to share the workload. When city officials understand what you are dealing with, they can provide more assistance. In smaller communities, such support often comes intuitively. In larger cities, you have to make these connections and make yourself available.

Finding allies in the business community

The business community can be a resource to you. After the Sandy Hook Elementary School shooting, a local company, GE Capital, offered a significant donation to the town of Newtown. Ultimately, instead of a financial donation, community leaders asked the company to provide an executive management team to assist in coordination between agencies, interfacing with media, and dealing with donations. While this agreement came several months after the incident, an arrangement like this could be very beneficial much earlier in your community.

➢ **Recognize that your leadership is vital even when another agency is in charge of the investigation.**

Your leadership role can become particularly challenging when another agency, such as the FBI, takes over the investigation of the incident. If that happens, keep in mind that the investigation is just one part of the community response and that you remain in charge of everything else. Federal agents will leave when the dust has settled. But this is your community, you will stay, and you have the community's long-term welfare in mind. It is important to your own resilience and that of your officers to push for respectful collaboration and an understanding that your continued leadership is crucial.

Tell the agency in charge of the investigation that it's important for you to be informed of any developments in a timely way. Keep your officers informed as the investigation unfolds, and try to ensure that they get updates before the information is released to the media. It's also important to articulate to your officers the important roles that you all will continue to play in supporting your community.

➢ **Stay alert to conflict within the agency.**

Some level of tension and conflict is inevitable within agencies that are managing the aftermath of a mass casualty event. You and your command staff should be alert to this and work proactively to address it. When there is conflict, even if it appears to be over trivial issues, it's important to not let it fester. Ignoring conflicts can be risky because these situations can lead to toxic group dynamics that quickly snowball out of control. Don't try to guess the root of a particular conflict; ask the officers what's going on and how to resolve the issue. You can't keep everyone happy all the time, but taking a collaborative approach will help you maintain positive working relationships in the long term.

> **Put your oxygen mask on first.**

After a mass casualty event, the chief is just as prone to mental health issues as officers. In addition, the pressure keeps piling on in these first few weeks: Your community is relying on you, your officers are relying on you, and the families of the victims are relying on you. Everyone needs you to hold it together and be the leader.

You can only carry on at this intensity for so long before you need some kind of safety valve to relieve the pressure. You need to have someone to talk to—it may be a friend, your spouse, a colleague, your mental health incident commander, or another mental health professional. Even if you're handling things fine, think of it as a proactive measure to prevent you from losing control at the wrong time. There are critical times (such as when you are interacting with the media) when you need to maintain composure, so it's important to find a private way to vent.

> **Model help-seeking behavior for officers.**

Consider whether it would be beneficial to disclose to your officers that you sought mental health support, even if it was just a check-in. You can keep the details to yourself, but letting your officers know that you took proactive steps to maintain your mental wellness will reassure those that really need it that it's okay to get help.

Nearly all the officers [who responded to the theater] chose to have separate private counseling with John or a member of his team. A very small number of officers declined to do the one-on-one sessions. I did not make them. They were all well aware that the psychological services were available. I tried to model my behavior by letting them know that I had gone for counseling, but I did not give an order that every officer go. Given all that they had been through, it didn't feel right to place this added pressure on them.

— *Daniel Oates, Chief of Police, Miami Beach, Florida,*
and former Chief of Police, Aurora, Colorado

---

7. The First Months

Managing challenges for your agency and your community

One thing that chiefs who experienced mass casualty events told us they did not expect was the intensity and duration of the aftermath. Several weeks after the event, you may expect the workload to become manageable again, but it may not do so. On top of managing the normal calls for service, your agency will likely continue dealing with an array of issues related to the incident for weeks or months.

> ➢ **Work with survivors and families to respectfully clean up temporary memorials.**

The good news is that many of the well-wishers may have gone home by now. There will still be events that you need to plan for such as candlelight vigils and fundraising runs, but there may be less chaos in the streets.

The bad news is that they may leave a lot of things behind. You will have to thoughtfully manage issues like how to remove thousands of stuffed animals from a makeshift memorial in a respectful, meaningful way and where to store all the keepsakes that families don't want. Involve survivors in the process of handling makeshift memorials once they become a hazard. You can arrange for the survivors to visit the memorial (away from the media) so they can take home whatever they want to keep before you remove the rest.

> ➢ **Call on volunteers to sort donations.**

Where do you send excess donations? When victims and their families receive an overwhelming volume of mail, how do you screen out death threats or painful reminders of their loss while ensuring they do receive the good wishes and support? Consider assembling a team of volunteers to screen mail and sort donations. Reach out to established aid organizations to identify places to send excess donations.

> ➢ **Be aware that investigations and reports can reopen the wounds.**

In addition to the criminal investigation, there will likely be any number of other investigations and reports stemming from the incident. An extreme example is the Sandy Hook Elementary School shooting, which resulted in half a dozen reports from state and federal agencies. Each new report can reignite the media storm. Investigations may bring to light new details about the perpetrator, the emergency response, or the victims. Reliving these events, especially when new information causes officers to question their actions, can reopen wounds that may just be starting to heal and can pile on the guilt.

A mass casualty event can shake up a community's sense of safety and spark new conversations about how to improve safety going forward. This may result in the community requesting or demanding more police presence in some settings. For example, after the Sandy Hook Elementary School shooting, the community was particularly concerned about school safety, and the Newtown Police Department committed to assigning officers or security guards full time to every school in the community.

Your agency cannot take on new responsibilities without new resources. Work with other community leaders to ensure you have the resources to meet these needs in the long term.

Managing challenges and stressors for officers

> **Be aware of emotional exhaustion.**

When an officer smiles at a pedestrian just after being berated by a driver during a traffic stop, the effort to experience and deflect another person's emotions is called *emotional labor*. Professionalism and courtesy often demand that you perform within a set of rules about how you express yourself regardless of what happened earlier or how you may be feeling inside. Your officers perform this way constantly—expressing sympathy when families need comfort, providing stability when others are falling apart, or expressing hope when the community wants to feel that something good can come out of this tragedy.

This is an important part of the role police play in the community, but over time it becomes exhausting. Without breaks it can become more difficult for officers to deal with their own reactions in a healthy way. Make sure officers have time and space to meet their own needs.

> "Everything changed after the incident. There was no more idle chatter in the hallways, and employees—both officers and dispatchers—were keeping to themselves more. Daily briefings, which were once vibrant interactions between shifts, had become solemn events."
>
> — *Marc Montminy, Chief of Police, Manchester, Connecticut*

> **Be aware that serious mental health problems can emerge now, just as things are getting back to normal.**

Sometimes when the initial response to an event ends, the acute stress that officers feel subsides. As the workload dies down, officers finally have some time to notice and deal with their own reactions to the event. Some people start to bounce back, and others have more difficulty coping. However, there's not a strict timeline; it's not uncommon for serious mental health problems to emerge months or even years after a traumatic event.

Many officers will not recognize signs of a lasting mental health problem, and they might not always be evident at work. Instead, they might have problems with their spouse or start drinking heavily.

> **Keep working closely with your mental health team.**

When the media is gone, the funerals are over, and the investigation is complete—in other words, when the immediate stressors slow down—your mental health team starts shifting gears. This is the time to check in again and catch officers who are not finding effective coping mechanisms and to start looking for colleagues who are starting to develop more serious problems. It is important to collaborate closely with your mental health team to recognize potential challenges early on and resolve them sensibly.

> **Anticipate trauma triggers, and prepare officers to deal with them.**

Trauma triggers—experiences that remind an individual of the event and can trigger a return to the memories and feelings associated with the event—are everywhere. It's impossible to avoid all trauma triggers, but it is possible to anticipate some of them and educate officers about how to deal with them.

Managing trauma triggers in Newtown

About five months after the tragedy at Sandy Hook Elementary School, Newtown's Chief Michael Kehoe scheduled a full departmental meeting and invited his behavioral health team to participate and talk about what triggers traumatic memory and what to do when it happens. An officer then approached the therapists about the upcoming recertifications at the shooting range. Couldn't that be a trigger?

The mental health team knew that one of the first senses activated for the responders at Sandy Hook was olfactory. The smell of gunpowder at the scene was overpowering. For all the Newtown officers engaged at Sandy Hook, recertification at the range would be the first time on duty that they would smell gunpowder again.

A plan was drawn up quickly:

- Officers were informed that requalifying on the range as well as the smell of gunpowder may act as a trigger. This was done during roll calls where a mental health team member briefly talked about possible triggers.

- Any interested officer could go to the range and practice prior to recertification. This was voluntary and could be done one-on-one.

- Should there be a negative experience from recertifying, officers were encouraged to either contact a therapist they had previously worked with or get in touch with a mental health provider on the team.

> **Create a long-term officer wellness plan.**

In chapter 2, we described strategies for creating an officer wellness committee and engaging your officers and mental health staff in a making a long-term wellness plan. Make it clear that officer wellness is still a priority, and convene your committee to develop a plan for the years ahead.

If you haven't done so already, make basic education about mental wellness a part of officer training. Officers need to know the basics of trauma and trauma triggers, healthy and unhealthy coping mechanisms, and where to get support.

> **Ensure officers have access to evidence-based services and supports.**

If an officer needs mental health care for a serious mental health condition, they should work with a mental health professional who is experienced at diagnosing addiction and trauma-related disorders. This is important even if it seems clear that the officer has a specific diagnosis, because trauma-related disorders can closely resemble one another. It is also very common for individuals who experience such traumatic events to have more than one diagnosis.

While your agency may not be directly responsible for providing mental health services, your mental health incident commander should know which services are effective in treating common mental health conditions resulting from trauma so he or she can help connect officers to appropriate services.

Officers should have access to an array of providers who have experience with evidence-based treatments, including

- medication management;

- exposure therapy;

- cognitive-behavioral therapy;

- eye-movement desensitization and reprocessing (EMDR);

- accelerated resolution therapy (ART);

- interpersonal therapy;

- medication management for addictions;

- integrated, concurrent treatment of addiction and other mental health conditions.

Any inpatient psychiatric or addiction treatment should be provided by institutions or individual providers with experience and sensitivity working with traumatized individuals.

Unfortunately, not all mental health professionals are trained in effective practices, and many are not familiar with the effects of trauma. The U.S. Department of Veterans Affairs National Center for PTSD offers sound guidance on finding a trauma-informed therapist at http://www.ptsd.va.gov/. The Substance Abuse and Mental Health Services Administration (SAMHSA) can also help officers find treatment providers at https://findtreatment.samhsa.gov/ or 800-662-HELP (4357).

> **Consider setting up a formal peer support network.**

Most officers have an easier time talking to a fellow officer than reaching out to a professional; it makes sense for those peers to be trained to help fellow officers access professional mental health supports if needed. And a peer support program can help officers learn how to look out for their colleagues. For an example of how a peer support program works, see the case study of New York City's Police Organization Providing Peer Assistance (POPPA) program on page 27. Your agency may not be able to replicate the scale of POPPA, but the principles may be helpful, and you may have greater capacity by joining together with law enforcement agencies around your region or state.

> **Continue education and outreach to officers' families.**

Spouses and families often recognize a serious mental health problem before the officer does. They need guidance on how to help their loved one get needed support. Your mental health manager should continue to reach out proactively to communicate with officers' families.

Managing leadership challenges

> ➤ **Adjust your expectations, and get help if the intensity does not let up.**

Police officers do not become chiefs without ambition, and no one with ambition has plenty of free time to take on a whole new job. Yet the direct demands from mass casualty events, together with the barrage of offers to help and requests for information, can easily become a second full-time job.

Some chiefs may be able to juggle some of these demands by developing greater efficiency, temporarily working more hours, or delegating effectively to people with the requisite skills. Ultimately, the increased demands may dictate that you change the structure of your agency or bring in new personnel to deal with new responsibilities.

The increased workload comes at the same time as you are dealing with a high level of scrutiny—from the media, your community, and your officers. It is a challenge knowing that any missteps you make will be noticed immediately and judged harshly.

Several weeks out, you may feel exhausted. Most chiefs will have times when they feel overwhelmed and ineffective. You will be more likely to manage your frustration or disappointment if you remember that there is no such thing as a perfect response to large-scale trauma and accept, even expect, that there will be missteps. You will be able to cope better if you adjust your expectations about things returning to "normal" and accept that you will instead reach a new normal someday.

> My aim every day was to come to work and move the agency forward. For a whole year I could not do that.
>
> — *Michael Kehoe, Chief of Police (ret.), Newtown, Connecticut*

> ➤ **Help officers move forward by acknowledging the toll the event has taken on you.**

"Emotional labor," described on page 88, is a good description for the job of a police chief in the first months after a mass casualty event. Aside from your own emotional reaction to the event itself and the frenzy of work demands that follow, you must also process the emotional tugs of others who are having an intense reaction to the event.

In normal circumstances, chiefs may be spared some emotional labor by the law enforcement culture that values stoicism, self-reliance, and compartmentalization of emotional reactions. But mass casualty events are not normal circumstances, and these coping strategies may not work when agencies are challenged with the intense emotions that follow such events. For better or for worse, group dynamics often cause leaders to become focal points for the fear, anger, aspirations, and grief of their followers.

As chief, you can expect to become the target of hostility or unfair criticism for matters that were beyond your control. Alternatively, you may be lauded individually as a hero because of the collective efforts of all first responders. Try not to take it personally.

This intensity of emotion is why police chiefs may find it useful to acknowledge some of their own reactions in the first weeks after the event. Most officers will appreciate an acknowledgment that this is a difficult time for everyone and that you, like everyone else, have strong feelings.

Although encouraging officers to be more emotionally aware may seem like opening a can of worms that will only make things worse, the opposite is probably true. Officers will appreciate your acknowledgment, but most officers will prefer to discuss such personal experiences outside of the work setting. By being open with officers about the feelings that stem from the event, you can decrease the risk that their emotions will leak out in other ways—such as in anger toward fellow officers or agency leadership.

> For better or for worse, group dynamics often cause leaders to become focal points for the fear, anger, aspirations, and grief of their followers.

Tips for helping officers to heal

Be flexible. Running a tight agency is important, but after a mass casualty event, it is temporarily more important to bend the rules on a case-by-case basis and give your officers the time and space they may need. For example, after the Sandy Hook Elementary School shooting (which occurred in December 2012), Chief Kehoe rolled vacation time that would have expired at the end of the year to the new year, because most officers had not been able to take planned vacation.

Be supportive. You cannot be there for everyone all the time, but you can make sure someone is. Encourage officers to take care of themselves and take time off if needed. Make it clear to your officers that their well-being is a priority.

Be transparent. If you have struggled with the emotional impact of an incident you responded to or if you had to seek help, mention it. You don't have to go into the details, but acknowledging that you have sought mental health support can validate your officers' decision to do so themselves.

Connect survivors and cops. This can be a powerful way to help officers process the events and find support. Chiefs recommend bringing together survivors, cops, other first responders, and even hospital personnel for a breakfast or lunch. Spending time with others who have been through the same traumatic event builds community and resilience.

Allow officers time with families at the memorial site. Being able to mourn alongside families can also be a useful way for officers to process their experience.

Limit officers' exposure to triggering events. It will be hard to avoid reminders of the incident, but you can help by not mandating that officers participate in events where they will hear the stories and see the images again. That means thinking carefully about how many officers need to read the latest report and who needs to review news articles or attend an award ceremony. Delay tactical debriefings as long as possible, and do not use the event as an example in officer training.

8. The Long Haul

Managing challenges for your agency and your community

A mass casualty event will continue to shape your community and your agency for years to come. Some high-profile events become so embedded in our nation's culture that strangers, hearing where you are from, will think first of the event. When you say "Columbine" or "Sandy Hook," everyone has some image or memory of those events. It may be hard for your community to move forward on its own terms.

In the years after the event, your community will relive what happened in a variety of ways. These reminders can be therapeutic and healing, or they can be upsetting reminders of the darkest days. As chief of police, you can bring together other community leaders and help lead the community in healing.

> ➤ **Try to make anniversaries a healing event rather than a painful reminder.**

Anniversaries are key days in the process of individual and collective healing after trauma. They are always both painful reminders of the tragedy and moments when the community can come together and create meaningful, helpful ways to commemorate the unforgettable. The first anniversary is often the hardest.

How Newtown managed the first anniversary of Sandy Hook

In preparation for the first anniversary of the Sandy Hook Elementary School shooting, the town of Newtown decided to ask all media representatives and well-wishers to stay away from the town on the day of the first anniversary. The strategy was designed to meet the needs of the community and the families who had suffered the most; they did not want to expose their sorrow and healing to onlookers.

Instead, the community tried to involve people touched by the tragedy in the way families wanted their loved ones to be remembered: by conducting an act of kindness. People who wanted to honor the victims could share an act of kindness with a person they know, a stranger on the street, or their community. A week before the anniversary, key people in the community explained the concept to media in press briefings staged by the media relations staff of GE Capital. It worked; the TV trucks and visitors stayed away, and the community was able to commemorate the victims away from cameras and public scrutiny.

In recent years, communities affected by mass shootings have learned not to let their community be overrun by media and well-wishers on this important day but instead to take control of what they want the day to be like. In addition to controlling the media presence, communities have planned events like wellness fairs, conferences, and commemorations for the anniversary. The key to these events is that they are driven by the community's needs, not from pressure by outsiders.

> ➤ **Look for opportunities to help the community heal.**

Just as a traumatic event affects the whole community, healing is a long-term process that often involves the whole community. Communities, law enforcement agencies, and individual officers approach the healing process differently. For many, it helps to create some positive change, such as working to prevent further violence, supporting a charity favored by survivors or victims' family members, or simply coming together as a community. You and your officers can benefit from leading or joining in something positive.

Is there a cause that the community can get behind or a service you can do for the survivors? Are there ways you can help everyone feel safe?

Oak Creek: Coming together to address hate

The Sikh Temple shooting in Oak Creek, Wisconsin, targeted a religious minority. While the event obviously deeply affected the Sikh community, it also galvanized the broader community to support them as documented in the film *Waking in Oak Creek*.[*] Among other activities, the police chief and the Sikh community successfully advocated with Congress to have Sikhs added to federal hate crime forms so that crimes against that community would be tallied in their own category rather than "other." The community also joined Not In Our Town, a national movement to stop hate, address bullying, and build safe, inclusive communities.

––––––––––––––––––––––––––––

[*] Not in Our Town, *Waking in Oak Creek* (Washington, DC: Office of Community Oriented Policing Services, 2014), DVD, http://ric-zai-inc.com/ric.php?page=detail&id=COPS-CD044.

Moving the community forward after the Platte Canyon High School shooting

While not a mass casualty event, the Platte Canyon High School shooting offers an example of how the community (including law enforcement) can move forward in a positive direction after tragedy. During the incident, a gunman entered a high school in Bailey, Colorado, and took several female students hostage. After sexually assaulting several girls, he ultimately killed one, Emily Keyes. A few days later, on the same day as the memorial service for Keyes, 5,000 motorcyclists rode from Columbine to Platte Canyon in honor of the victims of both school shootings. The ride evolved into an annual parade, a 5K run, and the creation of the I Love U Guys Foundation, which advances collaboration between schools, first responders, and experts to improve school safety.

Managing challenges and stressors for officers

➤ **Be aware that time doesn't heal for everyone.**

There is a wide range of normal reactions to grief and trauma, and most people are resilient. The majority of officers who experience a traumatic event will not develop a serious mental health condition. But it can be hard to predict who will have difficulty months or years later. It is not uncommon for the reverberations of a mass shooting to continue past the first anniversary of the event. Even years later, major life changes such as divorces and career changes can stem from the incident. One challenge with such a delayed reaction may be that officers themselves don't necessarily recognize the connection between the incident and the difficulty they are having.

If an officer is struggling, it may seem to come out of the blue, or it may be hard to tie new behavior to the long-ago traumatic event. Many officers who experience problems like excessive drinking or changes in mood will be able to conceal that from colleagues for a long time.

> A couple years later, when an officer quits and says "I'm not getting paid enough for this," what they really mean is that they are no longer willing to absorb additional psychological trauma.
>
> — *Marc Montminy, Chief of Police, Manchester, Connecticut*

Serious warning signs of a mental health problem

Some serious warning signs indicate that an officer may need professional mental health evaluation, including the following:

- Expressing that life is not worth living or that it would be better if they were dead

- Intoxication at work or while driving

- Seeing or hearing things that other people cannot see or hear

- Severe fatigue, drowsiness, irritability, or anger that interfere with the ability to work or drive

---

> ➢ **Anticipate triggering events, and provide support.**

Trials, anniversaries, and other events can bring an officer back to the fight-or-flight reaction they experienced during the incident. Officers may be particularly frustrated because they already dealt with the event and feel like they are back to square one. Some officers who seemed to handle the initial incident without problems may have a strong reaction to triggering events.

The good news is that most officers who dealt with the incident before have the skills to deal with triggering events as well, especially if they have easy access to mental health support. With predictable triggering events, it may be possible for officers to avoid the worst exposure—to decide not to follow the news reports of the trial, for example, or not to read a new investigative report. Officers should also have the flexibility to prepare for triggering events—to take vacation days, schedule extra time with family or friends, get mental health support, or spend time with fellow officers.

With these events, it can be helpful to anticipate that some officers will struggle and to reach out to them proactively. Work with your mental health team on a strategy for addressing predictable triggering events.

Help officers cope with the trial.

Trials can be especially difficult for officers. They may need to testify to the events they witnessed, reliving the incident in great detail. The media attention on the police response may return. After the trial, a flood of information that could not be released previously may be made available to the media, reigniting the media's interest in the perpetrator, the police response, the victims, or other issues.

The verdict and sentencing portion of a trial can be stressful and sometimes disappointing. Many people hope that a guilty verdict or the harshest possible sentence will help bring them closure, but this is not always the case. Officers may be frustrated when the sentence does not bring the relief they hoped for.

How mental health support helped Aurora officers cope with the trial

The trial of the perpetrator in the Aurora Century 16 theater shooting came almost three years after the event. The Aurora police chief and police psychologists working with his department anticipated that the trial would be difficult for officers, especially those who would testify. They compiled a list of all the officers who were testifying, and police psychologists reached out to each officer. Each officer was required to have a check-in with a mental health professional so that no one was singled out for seeking assistance.

Anticipate the impact of other mass casualty events.

Mass casualty events, especially mass shootings, can quickly take over the news cycle. When another incident occurs, officers may be triggered by news stories or images of the event. This is especially true if the incident is similar to their experience in some way—e.g., the same type of victims or the same type of location.

➢ **Support officers in finding their own ways to remember and cope.**

On the first anniversary of Columbine, I was sitting on my deck, alone with a glass of whiskey. . . . After the Platte Canyon shooting, I didn't want any of my guys to go through a dark night, sitting alone, drinking alone, when they don't have to. So we organized a 38-mile run from Jeffco Sheriff's to Platte Canyon High School—the first 35 miles were just for the guys who were in the school during the incident. The guys needed to be together, grieve together, and have some time. It was hugely cathartic—we can laugh and cry together, acknowledging that we are human, acknowledging that we are a year out, and it is still an important thing. We still do a 5k every year with some of the guys who were on the entry team.

— *Sergeant AJ DeAndrea, Patrol Officer, Arvada, Colorado, and an entry team leader at the Columbine and Platte Canyon High School shootings*

Officers will come up with their own plans for commemorating the anniversary or other significant markers of the event. For example, the officers who were first on scene may want to get together to honor the victims. Try to support them, or at a minimum don't do anything to stop them. Unlike awards, which may unnecessarily or artificially single out groups of responders, these informal gatherings can serve an important function for those who feel they share a common experience. The key is that they come from officers and are entirely voluntary.

If you find out that a group of officers is planning an event on an anniversary, consider whether to plan a separate, optional commemoration for the entire agency. Many staff will certainly want some acknowledgment of the day.

> ### ➤ Create a long-term infrastructure to support officer mental health.

In order for officer mental wellness to stay a priority within your agency, you will need to institutionalize new policies around psychological services and programs to support officer wellness. We suggest making the following a permanent part of your agency's structure:

- The mental health manager role
- An officer wellness workgroup
- Officer wellness education and training
- Regular interaction with mental health professionals

For more information about how to do this, return to chapter 2.

Managing leadership challenges

> ### ➤ Attend to your own mental wellness.

To maintain ongoing support for your officers and your community, it is important that you as the chief continue to attend to your own mental wellness. Are you constantly stressed or have you started to feel disconnected from your work or home life? Do you have the allies and supports you need to move forward and be successful in your role as chief? These aren't easy questions, so take time to get support from friends, family, fellow chiefs, and mental health professionals.

> ### ➤ Be wary of defining yourself by your crisis leadership.

You may have been in your element during the crisis or you may have felt you made too many mistakes. Either way, be wary of going through life defining yourself by how you performed during this crisis. If you become too attached to this identity, you might find the rest of your day-to-day life just doesn't feel important or that you are out of step with a wider community that has moved on.

If this happens, try to reconnect to the people and activities that were most important to you before the crisis. Or seek out mental health support to define your next steps.

Like your officers and your community, you have been through a traumatic experience. After traumatic experiences most people re-evaluate their lives and reconsider their priorities. Think of the experience like a heart attack—after a heart attack, you have an opportunity to reassess how you want to go forward. You may make a new commitment to exercise or diet or end a bad marriage or finally get your master's degree. Reassessment is a helpful process after an incident. You may find yourself with changing priorities and ambitions, and this is entirely normal.

You might find yourself with renewed energy for your position as chief and be excited to take on new initiatives to advance public safety in your community. You might decide to switch careers and pursue a long-held ambition. Or the incident may have opened your eyes to an important issue, and you may begin dedicating yourself to charity or advocacy work. You might decide to move to get away from constant reminders of the tragedy. This process is not about reinventing yourself so much as it is about making meaning out of your experience and making the best of the new things you learned about yourself. How can you best use your talents? What would ensure your long-term happiness? Do you want something good to come out of what you've endured, and how can you contribute to that?

One way to work through these questions is to contact mentors or colleagues, especially chiefs who have been through a similar crisis. Look for advice from someone you consider wise and thoughtful rather than someone who is still struggling.

If you decide to transition out of your current role, give sufficient notice for others to adjust and work with your command staff and community leaders on a plan that helps everyone through the process.

However you move forward, know that there is a growing community of chiefs who have been through these mass casualty events. They may be able to support you and provide perspective on how to plan your future.

HANDOUTS AND OTHER RESOURCES

To help your officers understand the importance of mental wellness and the impact that trauma can have on them, you may wish to share some personal accounts or information. The resources in this section are designed to be copied and handed out for educational purposes. You may find that they are slightly repetitive; this is deliberate. People learn in different ways, and where one person might get a lot out of personal accounts, others will appreciate a more systematic description of how acute trauma affects the body.

Chief Edwards' Story: Overcoming PTSD

John Edwards is the chief of police in Oak Creek, Wisconsin. He oversaw the police response to the 2012 shooting at the Sikh Temple of Wisconsin, where a white supremacist killed six worshippers and injured four others, including a police officer.

In 1989, I had been on the job for four years. One night, I was working the third shift when I came across an individual at a truck stop off the interstate. There was a car in a back area, where I would normally run into prostitutes, and I saw two people in the backseat.

When I saw the car, I felt something was wrong. They train us to trust the hairs on the back of our necks. I started to walk around the car, and I saw an Indiana plate. I knew immediately who it was. The FBI was looking for an escaped prisoner who had tried to shoot a sheriff's deputy in Indiana and taken a hostage before fleeing north with a prison employee who helped him escape.

As I was walking around the car, the driver got out of the backseat and came around the other side with two guns. He shouted, "Put your hands up! Get on the ground! Get on the ground!" Later on, when interviewed, he admitted that his plan was to get me on the ground, handcuff me, and then execute me.

> They said if he'd been trying to kill me, he would have hit me more than twice.

I decided not to lie down on the ground. I had my hands raised, and I knew the gun would not penetrate my vest. I was young and agile, so I turned, put my head down, and ran. I knew I would get shot in the back. A bullet went through my jacket and my badge. Another hit me in the hand, which threw me off balance. I got behind a car, and I took my gun out to engage him. But he was already in the car, leaning out the open window and pointing his guns back in my direction. I was going to shoot him, but I saw two people just behind him at the gas station in the line of fire, so I ran to my car and chased him on the expressway, into the next county south.

He and his accomplice stopped at a farm and holed up in a barn. His accomplice was a psychiatrist, and she had medication on her. They both took medication and overdosed. When they were found, they were unconscious but alive.

When he went to trial, the jury found him guilty of reckless use of a weapon but not guilty of attempted murder. They said if he'd been trying to kill me, he would have hit me more than twice.

When these things happen, you either get angry, or you go into a shell. A doctor asked me later what I would have done if I had been able to stop them. I would have shot them both. That's not what you are supposed to do, but I was just so angry that they had tried to kill me.

Right afterward, I was at the hospital. There was nothing life-threatening about my injuries, but it hit me that I almost died. I went back to the police department, and they interviewed me right away. Later, we found out that my interview was completely wrong. I swore that the woman's hair was white blonde, and it was actually black. I got tunnel vision and focused on the gun. I could probably still tell you the serial number on that gun, but I got all the other details wrong. Now I know that there's an adrenaline dump during these incidents, and a rest period is needed to remember correctly.

Afterward, I was treated like a hero. I got a letter of commendation and an award ceremony. That was really hard because I knew I screwed up. I approached the car wrong. I didn't see his hands. The whole time I was thinking, "Shit, this is wrong. This is wrong." But I still did it. The hero label is a pretty heavy burden to put on somebody who knows they made a mistake.

When I got back to work after two months of medical leave, the chief called me into his office. The chief was a World War II vet, and his whole office was a memorial to World War II. He said, "I always like to talk to someone who has tasted a bit of the lead. You hear about these doctors, but you don't need doctors. You just need to suck it up."

So I did. I sucked it up for about two years. I was paranoid on calls. I was hypersensitive. It got so bad that once an elderly man asked me to unlock his car for him, and I made him stand 50 feet away.

I couldn't sleep. Once, my wife moved in her sleep, and I jumped up on top of her and grabbed her by the throat.

I couldn't sleep. Once, my wife moved in her sleep, and I jumped up on top of her and grabbed her by the throat.

When a new chief came in, I decided I couldn't take it anymore. I told him I needed help, that I had to go see someone. He took my gun and badge away for seven months. He said he wasn't letting anyone get a disability on his watch. I had just gotten married, and my wife was pregnant.

I went to several doctors, and they all said, "This guy isn't lying. He does have PTSD," but that wasn't enough for the chief. PTSD wasn't as well known back then. The mayor got wind of what the chief had done and intervened. I was finally able to get my job back and get reimbursed for all that time.

More than 20 years later, the Sikh Temple shooting brought back my PTSD. It was about two or three days after the shooting, and I went to the hospital to see Lieutenant Brian Murphy, the officer who was shot during the incident. His wife was sitting next to him in the hospital room. He couldn't communicate, so I took her out into the hallway and tried to explain the disability benefits to her. A few nights later, I woke up at 3 a.m., and my bed was soaked. I was sweating profusely, crying uncontrollably, shaking, and trembling, just like after my shooting. The scene of Brian in the hospital bed is what brought it all back. It was a snapshot of many years before when I was in the hospital after my shooting, my wife was in the chair next to me, and my sergeant came in to talk to me and my wife.

When I came into work, I called my captains into my office, and I broke down. I told them, "You cannot tell the officers; the supervisors can't know." But I wanted the captains to know so they could watch out for me.

The Milwaukee area has police officer support teams to assist officers after a critical incident. I called in a lieutenant from Milwaukee to come to one of my staff meetings and talk with the supervisors about what they were feeling. The room was very quiet. At that point, I felt that I had to tell them what had happened to me. I told them that I didn't want them to have to deal with that. It was important for them to know it's okay if it happens, and don't suck it up.

I went to see a psychologist who works with us at the police department. I spent about three hours talking, getting a tune-up. It reassured me and got me back on track.

One of the things I'm doing now is trying to create a branch of the city employee assistance provider (EAP) to provide six visits to a psychologist or psychiatrist for police- and fire-related PTSD. The city pays for it, but they don't look at the medical records. This is not part of the disability determination process, and we control the network of doctors, so we know that officers can't use it to game the system. The goal is that early intervention can make it not as severe as it was for me and can prevent worker's comp claims down the line.

Lori Kehoe's Story: The Impact of Trauma on Law Enforcement Spouses

Lori Kehoe, RN, is a former hospice nurse and advocate for her adult son with special needs. Lori is also the wife of Chief Michael Kehoe, ret., who oversaw the police response to the 2012 Sandy Hook school shooting in Newtown, Connecticut.

December 14, 2012, the day of the Sandy Hook school shooting, was very long. I did not expect Mike to come home that night. After all, they had cots at the police department; they had uniforms and showers. When he did arrive home at midnight, he talked and talked until he passed out in the middle of a sentence. At 6:00 a.m., he was out the door. I offered to answer phones or e-mail. His answer was "no, I got it covered." I offered to make him breakfast, and the answer—which became a common phrase in our home—was "no, I got it covered." It was rare that he needed me for anything.

This became the schedule: 6:00 a.m. to midnight. Mike was not available to talk on the phone, so our time was from midnight to two in the morning, when he would talk and tell me every little detail of the day. Each night it was necessary for Mike to decompress, and I saw it as my job to be available and to listen and do whatever he needed. He would continue to literally fall asleep talking. When Mike started yelling in his sleep, I could tell he was reliving the incident. This schedule lasted for about four months, and it became extremely isolating.

> Each night it was necessary for Mike to decompress, and I saw it as my job to be available and to listen and do whatever he needed.

Many family and friends were supportive, but a lot of people couldn't deal with the trauma. They would break down crying on the phone. Or people were afraid to call because they didn't want to intrude. And the last thing you want to do when something dramatic like this happens is dump it all on someone who can't handle it. I relied on the people who called me to be my support system, because I didn't dare reach out. I was isolated but, at the same time, saturated with the media. Newtown was on the news for three or four days straight. You couldn't turn on the TV without seeing it.

Mike does not get upset. He is always cool, calm, and collected. He doesn't bounce off the walls. A few weeks after the shooting, he came home and was pacing and absolutely agitated beyond agitated. He was concerned about his officers committing suicide. He expressed his concerns, and we came up with options for him to execute the next day. I was always the sounding board, bringing whatever common sense I could muster to the table.

Those were the days when I would wonder, whom do you call for answers? After all, isn't there always someone to call for help in life? When you got a flat tire, you call your dad. If your cake won't rise, you call your mom. I realized there is *no one* to call when 20 children get blown away in your town. You're watching your partner struggle with all these questions and no answers.

After 20 years as a hospice nurse, I understand grief and crisis. Without that experience, we probably wouldn't still be married. Understanding the process of grief, I was able to identify a little anger this week, depression the next, bargaining, denial. Recognizing those stages allowed me to give Mike all the room he needed and understand the changes that were happening.

He was suddenly in control of everything. All of a sudden, he was telling me what to do and when. It was bizarre from a man who never gave orders at home. Then I realized he needed to be in control, to maintain order. He was spending his days making rapid-fire decisions continuously for weeks on end.

I went to the police department the day after the event. When I got off the highway, life changed. There was an officer and his town car on every corner for the entire length of the town—hundreds of officers in a little quaint country one-horse town, where they usually had no more than five officers on a shift. The police department was inundated with flowers, food, and gifts—so much that they almost couldn't do their jobs. Then I knew why he had everything covered: I suppose if you had 5,000 cops at your beck and call, you'd have it covered too.

> Recognizing those stages [of grief] allowed me to give Mike all the room he needed and understand the changes that were happening.

Finally in August (nine months after the shooting), Mike came home and said, "I got to something on my desk today that was on my desk before December 14." I thought to myself, "It's August, and the trauma is finally over."

A year after the shooting, I was mentally and emotionally not functioning, almost to the point of not getting out of bed. And even though I'm a nurse, I didn't know about trauma—I didn't know what trauma could do to a person or that there was such a thing as PTSD by association. I was so angry. I was mad at everyone and everything. I was depressed beyond belief, alone, and isolated.

The first anniversary was a turning point. The media stayed away, and I realized it was going to start simmering down. I realized it was not my job to take care of Mike any longer. So I went online and googled "law enforcement spouses and trauma," and I found a treatment center called the West Coast Post-Trauma Retreat in California. They had a week-long spouses' treatment program a couple of times a year.

I called them expecting them to turn me down because Newtown was such a large incident—I didn't want my trauma to overshadow someone else's. Instead, they interviewed me on the phone and said,

"It sounds like you could use our help. Come on out." They taught me that the trauma actually changes your brain—you can see it on an MRI. In addition to five full days of intervention and counseling, they did a physical treatment on me called eye movement desensitization and reprocessing (EMDR). It's designed to reduce the emotion that goes with the thoughts about the traumatic experience. It was extremely effective.

The treatment was necessary, and it changed my life. I absolutely came back a new woman, and I got better and better after treatment. Today, we're good.

I think education is so important. If an incident like this affects the officer, it affects the family. They may never talk about it, but it's still happening. And in some ways, I was lucky—many people react to trauma with alcohol abuse and out of control behavior that creates chaos. That did not happen to my officer.

You need to know that when a trauma occurs, alcohol abuse, depression, and chaotic behaviors can be symptoms of PTSD. Whether it is the officer or the family member displaying symptoms, you need to know what it looks like and that it is a physical injury. There is treatment. You can and must do something about it.

Sgt. O'Hara's Story: Managing Cumulative PTSD and Helping to Prevent Officer Suicide

Andy O'Hara *is a former California Highway Patrol officer, and the founder of The Badge of Life, an organization of active and retired law enforcement officers dedicated to preventing law enforcement suicide.*

Rather than coming from one incident, my PTSD was cumulative. I compare all the things that happen on a regular basis in police work to bee stings: One is tolerable, but as they build up, the pain becomes overwhelming.

In the course of my career with the California Highway Patrol, I accumulated 24 years of traumatic experiences—11 years as a sergeant and the rest as a traffic officer. I spent most of my career on the road, so I saw accidents on a daily basis. Some were gruesome: decapitations and dismemberments. I heard a lot of screams, and honestly you become tired of them. I responded to murders and suicides, backing up our local police departments. I saw injured and abused children. I was assaulted.

Probably the biggest incident that finally triggered a full blown case of PTSD was when an officer of mine was killed. He wanted to work overtime, and I knew he was tired. He pleaded with me to work, and I didn't want him to, but I relented and let him. He fell asleep on his motorcycle. I responded to the scene and half of his head was missing.

> In police work, the opportunity for mistakes is pretty high, and they haunt you.

Cumulative PTSD can be difficult to treat because you've got so much to deal with. You get into feelings like guilt and self-blame. You've got mistakes—dirty little secrets and mistakes in judgment. Everybody makes mistakes. In police work, the opportunity for mistakes is pretty high, and they haunt you. You take a lot of responsibility for things that happen on the road. Officers think about how they might have prevented it, how they might have gotten there sooner. All the "what ifs" will kill you.

It all begins to compile and becomes a big bundle of yuck that catches up to you in nightmares, depression, and flashbacks.

After my officer died, I took the blame for it. I couldn't forgive myself. I went through crying spells. My temper flared at home and at work. It became explosive. I started having panic attacks and anxiety. I started withdrawing. I became almost agoraphobic. The flashbacks reached a point where I couldn't sleep. I tried alcohol as a coping technique, and it worked: I could sleep.

I was a closet drinker. At first, I always quit 8 to 10 hours before work, but eventually I became an alcoholic. I was starting to show up to work with the odor of alcohol on my breath. Ultimately, drinking just made it worse; I wasn't able to suppress the feelings with the alcohol.

I started to get scared of losing my career. And there was pressure from my wife. I knew I had to quit drinking, and when I did I felt worse because I didn't have the sedative effects of the alcohol to overcome the flashbacks and anxiety.

About a year later, I became suicidal and went into the hospital. I've been on meds and in therapy since then, and I eventually retired on disability.

> It never occurred to me to get into therapy during my career. . . . If I had gotten therapy back then, I might not have had to retire.

I've been able to manage my problems. You don't cure PTSD; you learn to manage it. I've been able to manage the depression, the flashbacks, and the problems sleeping. But I still get panic attacks and anxiety, especially in traffic and in crowds. I don't handle stress very well. When I was on patrol, I was the figure of calm; nothing could bother me. Today, even driving is a challenge for me.

After I had gone through a lot of recovery, I reflected back on things that I could have done to avoid the predicament I got into. It never occurred to me to get into therapy during my career; I had never even heard of therapy. But it works pretty well. If I had gotten therapy back then, I might not have had to retire.

I got to thinking about why officers don't try therapy or medication. There are officers suffering from anxiety and PTSD, and they are determined to suffer through it for the rest of their lives. I think in this day and age, when officers are being questioned on a lot of things (shootings, arrests, and brutality), a lot of that could be avoided through some good therapy. And I think people are scared of medication. Medication doesn't necessarily affect your ability to work, but officers don't know that.

Sgt. DiBona's Story: Using His Personal Struggles to Help Other Cops

Mark DiBona is a deputy sheriff in Central Florida and is on the board of directors of The Badge of Life, an organization of active and retired law enforcement officers dedicated to preventing law enforcement suicide.

It was my lifelong dream to be a cop, and I started on the job at age 21. I've been in law enforcement for 30 years and a supervisor for 17.

About eight years ago, I was going through some tough times at work. I wasn't getting along with my immediate supervisor. We were both alpha males, but we had completely different styles of working and supervision. He was hard headed and strict, and I tried to be approachable to my guys. I felt he was very disrespectful. We became argumentative, insulting each other. He told me I wasn't aggressive enough, that I had to be harder on my guys. I took things to heart. He gave me an evaluation of "below standards." I felt worthless, like maybe he was right, maybe this job wasn't for me anymore. I felt like I couldn't do anything right.

This went on for a few months. It affected me physically. I gained 40 pounds. I refused to shave. I started coming in with my uniform wrinkled. I didn't go to my wife for help. I thought, "If you aren't a cop, you don't understand." The stigma is if you show a weakness, if you say something's bothering you, they look at you like you are weak.

So all this is already happening, and one night I am at the fire station, and a woman pulls up in her car. She cried, "My baby isn't breathing!" Just before she pulled up, the firemen had gone out on a call, so I did CPR on the baby. It seemed like I did CPR for an hour.

The baby died. I went to the funeral and the wake. I started to get nightmares about him, like maybe I could have done better. I can still feel that baby in my arms.

I told my boss, and he said, "You were just doing your job," like it wasn't a big deal.

I started feeling more worthless. I had lots of nightmares, waking up in cold sweats. I started thinking about the baby that died, and all the other stuff came up too: the horrible crashes I've seen, the victims of sexual abuse, the victims of robbery, the bad guys, the friends who died in the line of duty. I thought, "I don't want to be a cop anymore because this line of work sucks." One night, it hit me: This job is not for me; I'm failing really fast. I tried to fight the thoughts, but I felt like I was drowning. I attempted suicide twice that night.

I got lucky. A car pulled up, and it was another cop. He talked me down. I went home because I couldn't go back to work that night. I was afraid of losing my job. I thought they would take away my gun and put me in the hospital.

I called a close friend in Boston. He said he wanted me to come up there to get help. I went to Massachusetts and got some therapy, and then I went back to Florida a week and half later. I bounced back and forth between therapists. It wasn't clicking because the therapist didn't have any police background. I didn't go to the employee assistance provider because they are countywide, not specialized to police. I just wasn't in my comfort zone.

It was a difficult time in my life. I saw a person in me that I'd never seen before. There's that Michael Jackson song, "The Man in the Mirror." When I looked in the mirror, I didn't like the guy I saw. I didn't like his looks; I didn't like him. I felt weak. I knew in my heart that something was wrong, but it was hard to accept when I was diagnosed.

I stopped going to therapy, and I started looking on online. I found fascinating articles about police mental health, suicide, stigma, and an organization called The Badge of Life. I never realized that support was out there. I had a friend, a fellow officer, who committed suicide, but I thought it was just a family problem.

I'm on medication, and it's helped me to focus.
I was concerned about the meds; could I still be a cop?
But I can; it's not a problem whatsoever.
I'm still an active deputy sheriff.

I started to go to a support group in central Florida, just cops talking to cops. I found a therapist who is a retired cop. During the course of all this, I got my marriage back on track. I felt guilty about the way I treated my wife, and I apologized. She had felt helpless. She was trying to get me help, and I wouldn't take the help.

I was diagnosed with PTSD and depression. I'm on medication, and it's helped me to focus. I was concerned about the meds; could I still be a cop? But I can; it's not a problem whatsoever. I'm still an active deputy sheriff.

I've never had a suicidal thought since. I still have the nightmares, just not as much as I used to. I just feel a lot better now. I lost the weight I gained. I don't let it ruin my everyday life, ruin my job, ruin my marriage. On the days when I feel down, I've learned to control that—the anxiety, depression, and PTSD.

The biggest problem I have now is the stigma. When I'm open about it, the guys look at me funny. But there are others; when they hear my story, they come up to me and say, "Can I talk to you for a second?" There's nothing better than helping another cop through the issues that I experienced.

I really enjoy my life now, when for years I didn't. I still love being a cop.

Too Much, Too Ugly: Understanding the Trauma Contamination for Law Enforcement Officers

by John Nicoletti, PhD, ABPP

What is trauma? How do we get it?

Trauma is exposure to an event that involves injury or death. This exposure can be direct (you are the victim) or vicarious (you are the responder or witness).

What are the types of trauma that affect law enforcement officers?

Too much, too ugly, too soon.

The defining aspect of this type of trauma is the rapid onset of events with little time for psychological preparation. An example is the Aurora Century 16 theater shooting, which left 12 dead and 70 injured in a matter of minutes.

Too much, too ugly, too long.

This happens when the law enforcement officer is experiencing prolonged exposure to trauma either as a victim or through staying too long in assignments such as child sexual abuse, crime scene investigation, or homicide investigations. Prolonged exposure depletes the mind and body's energy reserves, making it increasingly difficult to cope with and process stressors.

Too much, too ugly, too similar.

This happens when the law enforcement officer is a victim of or a responder to a traumatic event that is similar to a previous incident. It can also happen when the brain makes a connection between an event (the death of an infant, for example) and something similar in the officer's life (their own baby).

Too much, too ugly, too different.

This happens when the law enforcement officer is a victim of or a responder to an event that is unpredictable and outside their normal life experiences, such as a mass casualty event. It can also happen when a responder encounters an unfamiliar type of incident.

What does trauma do to us?

- Trauma causes intrusion based on either our sensory modalities or our thoughts. Sights, sounds, tastes, smells, and touches that remind you of the traumatic event can cause the event to come to life in your thoughts or senses.

- Trauma causes flashbacks.

- Trauma destroys our comfort zones and shatters our assumptions about how the world works. For example, children are not supposed to be killed at school, and massacres should not happen at movie theaters.

- Trauma deteriorates our physical well-being.

What can we do about a trauma reaction?

Get rid of it, or you will have to live with it!

- **View psychological trauma symptoms the same as physical symptoms**. If you cut your leg open with a chainsaw, you would never say, "This shouldn't be bothering me." If you are having a trauma reaction, don't think to yourself, "This shouldn't be bothering me." If you did not treat the cut from the chainsaw, you would eventually bleed out. If you don't treat the trauma reaction, you will eventually "bleed out" mentally. Get psychological treatment.

- **Talk about it or write about it**. Keep talking and writing until you feel that it has become a memory as opposed to a thought. A thought is always at the front of our awareness, whereas a memory sleeps until we wake it up. For example, what did you have for dinner last Friday night? It takes a moment to recall that, because it is saved in your brain as a memory.

- **Manage your "Book of the Dead."** Work through your reactions to these deaths so that you can keep them as memories but they don't have the power to "wake up" and wander around in your thoughts.

"This Shouldn't Be Bothering Me:" Common Myths about Police Officers' Responses to Traumatic Events

"I shouldn't be feeling this way. This shouldn't be bothering me."

Law enforcement officers are exposed to an extreme share of human violence, tragedy, and suffering. In the face of so much violence, law enforcement culture has developed its own stoicism: Don't be bothered; suck it up, or you can't do your job. Stay cool. Stay strong.

Emotional restraint is vital during a crisis, and to maintain it an individual often learns to desensitize to violence. It can be difficult to remain detached, however, when faced with an incident that is too similar to everyday experience, for example when an officer takes a child's death to heart because the victim is the same age as their own child. On the other hand, an incident that is very unusual can be unsettling, such as when an officer responds to a mass casualty event for the first time. Suddenly, officers who are accustomed to being restrained may find it difficult to hold in their response to the stressful encounter.

Not surprisingly, many officers feel something is wrong with them when they experience strong emotions after a traumatic incident. Yet those reactions are quite normal and involuntary. Resilience is not the absence of emotional reactions—it is the ability to process such natural responses and overcome the impact of a tragedy over time.

Expecting not to feel anything after witnessing and responding to an atrocity is like expecting not to bleed after an injury—it's not how human bodies work. If you accidentally cut yourself working with a saw, would you say, "I should not be bleeding?" No, you would get medical help. Psychologically speaking, if you are having a trauma symptom and say to yourself, "This should not be bothering me," you will allow yourself to bleed out emotionally. A more resilient way to handle the situation would be to say: "This is bothering me, and I need to do something to fix it."

Whether we like it or not, our bodies react to a traumatic event and it can trigger unexpected and often unwanted feelings. But just as we can attend to physical injuries, we can attend to our psychological reactions and recognize that immediate care prevents future complications.

"I should be able to handle this on my own."

When officers realize they are reacting in unexpected ways to an incident, most of them think they should be able to handle the issue on their own. They're police officers. They are trained in self-control and problem solving. Asking for help is seen as a sign of weakness.

Most people deal with traumatic events by talking to friends and family or commiserating with co-workers. But that can be hard for police officers; friends and family may not be able to relate to the officer's experiences, and talking about it can make them uneasy.

If you find yourself in this situation, you can think of meeting with a mental health professional the same way you think about any other expert consultation. The expert can help you assess whether your experiences are normal (they probably are) or might be a sign of a lasting problem. They can suggest strategies for processing these reactions so you can move on. And they can help identify when an immediate coping mechanism—such as burying yourself in work or drinking every night to fall asleep—could result in long-term problems.

Here is one way to think about it: When we break a bone, we don't think we should be able to handle it ourselves; we trust professionals who are trained in healing that kind of injury. Similarly, our psychological injuries heal faster and better when they benefit from professional care.

"I'm shaking. I have a knot in my stomach. This means I'm scared and weak."

It does not fit the common image of a competent, composed officer to be shaking after a stressful encounter or to have knots in the stomach—yet these are very common, normal physical reactions to a traumatic event. That's because mortal fear or other traumatic situations cause the body to flood with adrenaline. The response is called "fight or flight"—all nonessential systems in the body shut down so energy can be directed toward the systems needed to either fight or flee. This affects the body in several ways:

- Shaking, especially of the hands. Not enough blood and oxygen is going to the small muscles in the body, impairing their ability to function normally.

- Stomach butterflies. The overall shutdown of all nonessential systems includes the digestive system. Throughout the day, the digestive tract constantly moves and contracts. When this stops, it creates a sensation of butterflies or knots.

- Tunnel vision. The visual field narrows. Officers often express concern that they did not see certain aspects of a scene (e.g., a pedestrian walking by or a car driving by); however, they cannot control this physiological response. During a fight or flight experience, if you choose to fight, you generally only need to focus on the object that poses the biggest risk (a gun, a knife, etc.). If you choose flight, you only need to see the escape route. Tunnel vision focuses our attention on the maximum chance of survival.

- Tunnel hearing. As with tunnel vision, the brain focuses only on the sounds that it perceives as essential for survival and filters out anything extraneous. For example, officers may not hear someone shouting at them, or some shouts may sound muffled during a fight-or-flight situation.

- Amnesia. Research suggests that high levels of stress can negatively impact memory, particularly short-term memory for simple facts. When faced with fight-or-flight decisions, the brain is concerned with survival, not detail. For example, law enforcement investigators might ask officers how many rounds they fired during a critical incident, but some officers may not know because the brain was not concerned with bullet count; the brain was concerned with stopping the threat.

"I shouldn't be freaking out over something that happened weeks or months ago."

People often think that symptoms will show up right away after a traumatic event. That is true only for some people; others won't experience any symptoms for days or even weeks. They might think they are fine and then all of a sudden have nightmares or become moody, for example. There's nothing wrong with having a delayed response to an incident. Just be sure you seek assistance or use your healthy coping strategies whenever you do become aware that you are experiencing a reaction.

In addition to such sudden or delayed responses to a traumatic event, the impact can also be cumulative: Think of the slowly boiled frog that doesn't even know that it's being cooked until it's too late. When you are constantly exposed to trauma, it can start to feel "normal" and you may not be aware of the impact it is having on you. Friends and family members may notice small changes in you first. Try not to become defensive if they bring this to your attention. Let their perspective serve as an early warning sign to you that it might be time for a mental wellness check.

"Going to the shrink will jam me up."

Many officers think that seeking help from a mental health professional will negatively impact their career. They fear the chief will find out about a drinking problem or they will be found unfit for their jobs. They worry that their fellow officers will think they are too weak to deal with stress.

What most officers don't know is that there is a very strict line between fit-for-duty evaluations (which the agency will see) and mental health treatment details (which the agency will not have access to or even be aware of). In fact, when you see a licensed mental health professional for treatment either in private practice or through an employee assistance provider, they must keep all interactions confidential, or they risk losing their license. The only exceptions to this confidentiality rule are cases where reporting is required by law: when the patient poses a danger to him or herself or others or when there is a case of child or elder abuse.

So in reality, it is often the other way around: Not seeking treatment can slow down officers in their law enforcement career as post-traumatic stress disorder or alcoholism or other negative responses become harder to control. Getting timely, professional help, on the other hand, ensures you stay ready to engage and resilient in the long run.

The Mental Health Incident Commander's Role during the Immediate Response to a Mass Casualty Event

Who should be assigned to this role?

If your agency does not have a mental health incident commander, the chief should assign a trusted individual to this role as soon as possible. This can be a temporary assignment while you determine who would be best to serve in this role for the long-term. The most important characteristics are *credibility, openness to learning, and empathy*. Ideally, this is an individual who has

- familiarity with your agency and law enforcement culture;

- credibility with your officers;

- mental health training;

- connections with your local mental health community;

- an understanding of the impact of trauma and familiarity with Psychological First Aid.

> If your agency does not have a mental health incident commander, the chief should assign a trusted individual to this role as soon as possible.

The temporary incident commander can be a police psychologist, a licensed mental health professional, a certified employee assistance professional who is also a mental health professional, a member of your command staff, or a chief from a neighboring community.

Depending on the scope of the incident and the size of your agency, your mental health incident commander may need an assistant.

Responsibilities: Immediate incident response

Supporting officers	Supporting the chief and command staff
• Monitoring officers' behavior and verbalizations on scene to see if any officer needs immediate assistance • Connecting officers in distress with peer support or mental health professionals • Sharing information about available mental health services with officers and ensuring that every employee has the name and phone number of a licensed mental health professional or supervisor to call in case they need to talk • Updating officers about the status of mental health services—even if it is just reassurance that services will be made available • Ensuring that a mental health provider or supervisor checks in with all officers and civilian staff before the end of shift; anyone conducting these check-ins should receive a copy of the handout "How to Assist a Fellow Officer after a Critical Incident" on page 129 • Contacting an officer's family members if needed	• Briefing the chief and other command staff • Advising the chief and command staff on operational decisions that impact officer mental health: e.g., an assignment to work with victims' families (see "Prioritize support for victims and their families . . ." on page 58) or when to file reports (see "Immediate incident response checklist: Supporting officer wellness" on page 68) • Vetting and managing self-deployed mental health service providers—unfortunately, it's unlikely that self-deployed providers will be able to assist on the first day, but you can take their information for the future and ensure they don't disturb victims, their families, or officers

Responsibilities: The first weeks

Supporting officers	Supporting the chief and command staff
• Triaging to decide which personnel need mental health follow-up (see "Managing challenges and stressors for officers" beginning on page 76 in chapter 6)	• Working with command staff to identify appropriate mental health service providers, including continuing to vet self-deployed responders; for qualifications to look for in a mental health professional, see "Assign a mental health incident commander" on page 37
• Proactively sharing information about mental health supports with all agency personnel, including civilian personnel and officers who were off duty during the incident	• Continuing to advise the chief and command staff on operational decisions that affect officer mental health
• Maintaining an active presence at police stations and the investigation scene and continuously monitoring officers' behavior for signs of distress	• Providing personal support to the chief and command staff to ensure they are able to manage their stress
• Regularly updating officers on the status of mental health services that will be made available to them in the future	
• Reviewing potential stressors on the community and officers (see "Managing challenges for your agency and your community" beginning on page 69 in chapter 6)	
• Reaching out proactively to officers' families to share information about mental health supports	
• Educating officers about healthy strategies for coping with stress and trauma (e.g. sleep, exercise, time with family and friends)	
• Attending full departmental meetings to be available for questions on wellness and resiliency; this is also an opportunity for the chief to emphasize his or her commitment to wellness	

Long-term planning

After the early weeks of an incident, officer mental wellness should remain a top priority. The mental health incident commander should review pages 69–101 ("The First Weeks" through "The Long Haul") to begin the process of understanding stressors and challenges the agency will continue to face. In particular, he or she should anticipate trauma triggers that might affect officers (such as requalifying for firearms use or testifying at a trial) and take appropriate countermeasures. He or she should continue support and education for officers, their families, and the chief. And finally, the mental health incident commander leads the process of developing a long-term officer wellness plan.

How to Assist a Fellow Officer after a Critical Incident

A mental health professional, supervisor, or fellow officer should check in as soon as possible with any officer who has been involved in a traumatic incident. This conversation can be brief and doesn't require any specialized training—just common sense and genuine concern. Here are some steps you can take:

1. **Ensure safety.** Make sure that the officer is safe and uninjured. If the immediate threat has passed, ask if he or she needs medical care and provide reassurance of safety.

2. **Provide practical assistance.** Ask if there's any way you can help—food, water, a ride home, or a call to a family member.

3. **Offer to talk.** Let him or her know you are available to listen. For example, say, "That was an awful situation. I'm sorry you had to go through it. Do you want to talk?" If he or she does not want to talk, don't be surprised and don't push it.

4. **Listen attentively.** Some people will want to talk through what they experienced, and others will not. Don't worry about fixing the problem, and don't feel like you need to ask detailed follow-up questions.

5. **Reassure.** If the officer seems upset, reassure him or her that whatever reaction they are having is normal. You can also offer a hug. If they feel fine, that's also okay. Say, "There's nothing wrong with you. You are having a normal reaction to an abnormal situation."

6. **Make sure the officer gets home safely, and leave a number to call.** Before you leave, give the officer your phone number or the number of a 24-hour helpline—somewhere they can call day or night.

Dos and don'ts for supporting a fellow officer

Do	Don't
• Listen carefully. • Be patient and sit with him or her for a few minutes. • Encourage him or her to go home, get some sleep, eat, or call a friend. • Leave if asked to, but make sure to leave behind a phone number in case they want to talk later.	• Tell him or her to suck it up and get back to work. • Ask for details of the incident to satisfy your curiosity. • Get side-tracked telling a story about your own experience.

Resources

Medical literature

Brymer, Melissa, Anne Jacobs, Christopher Layne, et al. 2006. *Psychological First Aid: Field Operations Manual*. 2nd ed. Los Angeles: National Child Traumatic Stress Network. http://www.nctsn.org/sites/default/files/pfa/english/1-psyfirstaid_final_complete_manual.pdf.

Mind Tools. 2016. "Holmes and Rahe Stress Scale." Mind Tools Ltd. Accessed April 4, 2016. http://www.mindtools.com/pages/article/newTCS_82.htm.

Rose, Susanna C., Johnathan Bisson, Rachel Churchill, et al. 2002. "Psychological Debriefing for Preventing Post-Traumatic Stress Disorder (PTSD)." *Cochrane Database of Systematic Reviews* 2. doi:10.1002/14651858.CD000560.

Violanti, John. 2014. *Dying for the Job: Police Work Exposure and Health*. Springfield, IL: Charles C. Thomas.

Media resources

On the Media. "The Breaking News Consumer's Handbook." New York Public Radio. Last modified September 20, 2013. http://www.onthemedia.org/story/breaking-news-consumers-handbook-pdf/.

Police Executive Research Forum. 2013. *Social Media and Tactical Considerations for Law Enforcement*. Washington, DC: Office of Community Oriented Policing Services. http://ric-zai-inc.com/ric.php?page=detail&id=COPS-P261.

Mental wellness education and support

Blue LLC. 2014. *BLUE*. Vimeo video. Accessed April 4, 2016. https://vimeo.com/105565084.

DeHart, Ralph. 2014. "The Blue App." iTunes. https://itunes.apple.com/us/app/the-blue-app/id931490733?mt=8&ign-mpt=uo%3D4.

Ferreras, Jesse. 2015. "'You Are Not Alone': RCMP PTSD Video Aims to Raise Awareness." *The Huffington Post Canada*, August 11. http://m.huffpost.com/ca/entry/7973626?ir=Impact&ncid=fcbklnkushpmg00000054.

Gilmartin, Kevin. 2002. *Emotional Survival for Law Enforcement*. Tucson, AZ: E-S Press. http://emotionalsurvival.com/author.htm.

Cactus. 2015. "Man Therapy." Accessed April 4, 2016. http://mantherapy.org/.

Organizations

American Police Chaplains Association
http://www.americanpolicechaplain.org/

Badge of Life
http://www.badgeoflife.com/

**Boston Police Peer Support
    Unit Self-Check Quiz**
https://www.bostonpeersupportquiz.org/welco
    me.cfm

**Center for Officer Safety and Wellness,
    International Association of
    Chiefs of Police**
http://www.theiacp.org/CenterforOfficerSafety
    andWellness

Concerns of Police Survivors
http://www.nationalcops.org/

First Responder Support Network
http://www.frsn.org/

**HEART (Healing Emergency and
    Response Team) 9/11**
http://www.heart911.org/

International Conference of Police Chaplains
http://www.icpc4cops.org/

**International Critical Incident
    Stress Foundation**
http://www.icisf.org/

**International Society for
    Traumatic Stress Studies**
https://www.istss.org/

**National Center for PTSD,
    U.S. Department of Veteran Affairs**
http://www.ptsd.va.gov/

**National Institute of Mental Health,
    National Institutes of Health**
https://www.nimh.nih.gov

Police Executive Research Forum
http://www.policeforum.org/

**Police Officers Providing
    Peer Assistance (POPPA)**
http://www.poppanewyork.org/

Virginia Law Enforcement Assistance Program
http://valeap.org/

Key Word Index

About the Authors

Laura Usher is the manager, criminal justice, and advocacy with National Alliance on Mental Illness (NAMI). Usher served for eight years as NAMI's program manager for crisis intervention teams (CIT) and has assisted law enforcement agencies nationwide in improving responses to people in the community experiencing mental health crises. Usher is also the coauthor of numerous reports, including *Responding to Youth with Mental Health Needs: A CIT for Youth Implementation Manual, Grading the States 2009: A Report on America's Health Care System for Adults with Serious Mental Illness*, and *State Mental Health Cuts: The Continuing Crisis*. She has served on numerous advisory panels on policing and mental illness for the Police Executive Research Forum, the International Association of Chiefs of Police, the Substance Abuse and Mental Health Services Administration, and The Arc.

Stefanie Friedhoff is a German-American journalist. Her work has appeared in the *Boston Globe, Time Magazine, Frankfurter Allgemeine Zeitung,* and many other publications. From 2006 to 2014, Friedhoff ran a variety of programs at the Nieman Foundation for Journalism at Harvard University, including Nieman's Trauma Journalism Program. At Nieman, Friedhoff created major conferences[20] convening trauma experts, victims, law enforcement, journalists, and others involved in the lives of survivors to explore each other's roles—and the role of storytelling—in the aftermath of crime and disaster. Friedhoff teaches media literacy for victim advocates at the Massachusetts Victim Assistance Academy and is a media consultant to the Resiliency Center for Victims of the Boston Marathon bombings. Friedhoff was retained as an expert consultant to NAMI to coauthor this publication.

Sam Cochran retired as major with the Memphis (Tennessee) Police Department after developing the nation's first CIT program and serving as its coordinator for 20 years. Today, he assists law enforcement agencies across the United States, England, Australia, and Israel in building partnerships with the mental health system and in starting their own CIT programs. He is a national spokesperson on mental illness and policing issues and received the 2000 News Person of the Year Award from City University of New York John Jay College of Criminal Justice. NAMI has named an annual law enforcement advocacy award after Cochran. He was retained as an expert consultant to NAMI to coauthor this publication.

Anand Pandya, MD, is the cofounder of Disaster Psychiatry Outreach in Brooklyn, New York, and a National Institute of Mental Health-funded researcher on the predictors of depression in survivors of disasters. He has won numerous awards for his work in the field. He is a coeditor of two award-winning books on disaster psychiatry and author of numerous articles and book chapters on disaster psychiatry and mental health advocacy. He previously served on the board of directors of the Menninger Clinic in Houston, Texas, and he has served two terms as president of NAMI. Pandya was retained as an expert consultant to NAMI to coauthor this publication.

---

[20] See Melissa Ludtke, "The Conference: Covering Violence and Tragedy," NiemanReports, accessed April 6, 2016, http://niemanreports.org/articles/the-conference-covering-violence-and-tragedy/.

About NAMI

NAMI, the **National Alliance on Mental Illness**, is the nation's largest grassroots mental health organization dedicated to building better lives for the millions of Americans affected by mental illness.

What started as a small group of families gathered around a kitchen table in 1979 has blossomed into the nation's leading voice on mental health. Today, we are an association of hundreds of local affiliates, state organizations, and volunteers who work in your community to raise awareness and provide support and education that was not previously available to those in need.

What We Do

We educate. Offered in thousands of communities across America through our NAMI State Organizations and NAMI Affiliates, our education programs ensure hundreds of thousands of families, individuals, and educators get the support and information they need.

We advocate. NAMI shapes the national public policy landscape for people with mental illness and their families and provides grassroots volunteer leaders with the tools, resources, and skills necessary to save mental health in all states.

We listen. Our toll-free NAMI HelpLine allows us to respond personally to hundreds of thousands of requests each year, providing free referral, information, and support—a much-needed lifeline for many.

We lead. Public awareness events and activities including Mental Illness Awareness Week (MIAW), NAMIWalks, and other efforts successfully combat stigma and encourage understanding. NAMI works with reporters on a daily basis to make sure our country understands how important mental health is.

About the COPS Office

The **Office of Community Oriented Policing Services (COPS Office)** is the component of the U.S. Department of Justice responsible for advancing the practice of community policing by the nation's state, local, territorial, and tribal law enforcement agencies through information and grant resources.

Community policing begins with a commitment to building trust and mutual respect between police and communities. It supports public safety by encouraging all stakeholders to work together to address our nation's crime challenges. When police and communities collaborate, they more effectively address underlying issues, change negative behavioral patterns, and allocate resources.

Rather than simply responding to crime, community policing focuses on preventing it through strategic problem solving approaches based on collaboration. The COPS Office awards grants to hire community police and support the development and testing of innovative policing strategies. COPS Office funding also provides training and technical assistance to community members and local government leaders, as well as all levels of law enforcement.

Another source of COPS Office assistance is the Collaborative Reform Initiative for Technical Assistance (CRI-TA). Developed to advance community policing and ensure constitutional practices, CRI-TA is an independent, objective process for organizational transformation. It provides recommendations based on expert analysis of policies, practices, training, tactics, and accountability methods related to issues of concern.

Since 1994, the COPS Office has invested more than $14 billion to add community policing officers to the nation's streets, enhance crime fighting technology, support crime prevention initiatives, and provide training and technical assistance to help advance community policing.

- To date, the COPS Office has funded the hiring of approximately 127,000 additional officers by more than 13,000 of the nation's 18,000 law enforcement agencies in both small and large jurisdictions.

- Nearly 700,000 law enforcement personnel, community members, and government leaders have been trained through COPS Office-funded training organizations.

- To date, the COPS Office has distributed more than eight million topic-specific publications, training curricula, white papers, and resource CDs.

- The COPS Office also sponsors conferences, roundtables, and other forums focused on issues critical to law enforcement.

The COPS Office information resources, covering a wide range of community policing topics—from school and campus safety to gang violence—can be downloaded at www.cops.usdoj.gov. This website is also the grant application portal, providing access to online application forms.

Though most agencies have trained and equipped their officers for immediate response to mass casualties, few have prepared their personnel for the psychological fallout. Tragic events can have a profound effect on first responders, who may suffer emotional distress that lingers long afterward.

To help the Newtown (Connecticut) Police Department cope with the murder of 26 people, including 20 children, at Sandy Hook Elementary School, the COPS Office reached out to the National Alliance on Mental Illness (NAMI) to provide guidance. *Preparing for the Unimaginable* is the result of NAMI's work with Newtown's police chief, Michael Kehoe.

This unique publication offers expert advice and practical tips for helping officers to heal emotionally, managing the public, dealing with the media, building relationships with other first responder agencies, and much more. But what makes this handbook especially helpful are the personal contributions of four police chiefs and numerous officers who have lived through incidents such as these and shared their experiences.

COPS
Community Oriented Policing Services
U.S. Department of Justice

U.S. Department of Justice
Office of Community Oriented Policing Services
145 N Street NE
Washington, DC 20530

To obtain details about COPS Office programs, call the COPS Office Response Center at 800-421-6770.

Visit the COPS Office online at **www.cops.usdoj.gov**.

National Alliance on Mental Illness

National Alliance on Mental Illness
3803 N. Fairfax Drive
Suite 100
Arlington, VA 22203

Visit NAMI online at **www.nami.org**.

ISBN: 978-1-935676-90-4
e121529737
Published 2016